LIFE AND DEATH:
THE PILGRIMAGE OF THE SOUL

A.R.E. MEMBERSHIP SERIES

LIFE AND DEATH: THE PILGRIMAGE OF THE SOUL

by Harvey A. Green

ARE PRESS

ASSOCIATION FOR
RESEARCH AND
ENLIGHTENMENT

A.R.E. Press • Virginia Beach • Virginia

This book is dedicated to my wife Rae,
whose tender lovingkindness has
sustained me throughout time.

A.R.E. Press
Sixty-Eighth & Atlantic Avenue
P.O. Box 656
Virginia Beach, VA 23451-0656

Green, Harvey A.
 Life and death : the pilgrimage of the soul / by Harvey A.
Green.
  p.   cm.
 Includes bibliographical references (p. 131).
 ISBN 0-87604-404-6
 1. Future life. 2. Cayce, Edgar, 1877-1945. Edgar Cayce
readings. I. Title.
BF1311.F8G73   1998
133.9'01'3—dc21   97-35145

The A.R.E. Membership Series

This book, *Life and Death: The Pilgrimage of the Soul,* is another in a continuing series of books that is published by the Association for Research and Enlightenment, Inc., for individuals who are especially interested in their personal and spiritual growth and transformation.

The A.R.E. was founded in 1931 as a nonprofit organization to study, research, and disseminate information on holistic health, vocational guidance, spiritual growth, dreams, meditation, life after death, and dozens of other subjects. The A.R.E. continues its mission today, nurturing a worldwide membership with conferences, study groups, and a variety of publications—all aimed at helping seekers find paths that will lead to a more fulfilling life, mentally, physically, and spiritually. The hallmark of A.R.E.'s publications is to be helpful and hopeful.

Many of the books published by A.R.E. are available in bookstores throughout the world and all are available directly from the A.R.E.'s mail-order catalogs.

Three new books in this *A.R.E. Membership Series* are sent as gifts each year to individuals who are Sponsoring members or Life members of A.R.E. Each of the titles in this series will become available, in the year after initial publication, for purchase by individuals throughout the world who are interested in individual growth and transformation.

For more information about membership benefits of the nonprofit Association for Research and Enlightenment, Inc., please turn to the last page in this volume.

The A.R.E. Membership Series:

Contents

PREFACE

There are many things which death is and many more which it is not. In a series of letters written by my friend Barbara over an eighteen-month period while she was terminally ill, she found the one single word which best described the inevitable experience she was facing. The sum total of what she was experiencing she recognized as *change*. This observation made from her close proximity to death was as enlightening as it was profoundly simple. Whatever the experience is, the result is surely change. Death can best be described as the pivotal point of change.

This work is written for the single purpose of awakening in the reader a sense of his or her own immortality, through a better understanding of the continuity of life in all realms. Through illustration, explanation, and inspiration, it is hoped that this book will increase understanding of the continuity of life sufficiently to bridge the gap between life and death. To more fully comprehend the relationship of life as it exists in the material world and as it exists in spiritual realms, both must be viewed as part of a single experience. The two different expressions, life in the material realm and life in the spiritual, are not so much separated by death as they are connected by it. With such a view, we awaken in ourselves a sense of immortality which immeasurably enriches our lives in the earth.

In the chapters which follow we will begin with creation and observe the process. Upon this observation we will base what we are and will be. We will move closer and closer into materiality weaving a story with those threads we call patterns. The patterns we will refer to over and over again are expressed differently as we journey throughout creation. We hope to make it obvious to the reader that it is only the expression of the pattern which changes and not the pattern itself. It is important to here note that "patterns" in the context of this work are what we understand as conditions, causes, motives, or realities so basic to life that they radiate from the center of creation.

To take the reader on a journey of the soul, we will build successively upon the work being presented to discover other realms associated with materiality as well as our relationship to them. As we observe how differently the same patterns are expressed while we move through reality, we will come to realize that all that does change is form. Love, faith, hope, unity, creativity, individuality, and self-awareness are some of the basic patterns that exist throughout all creation. These patterns are, however, expressed differently as one moves from one level of reality to another. By understanding the different expressions of life we better understand life itself.

We are dealing with concepts that are difficult, if not impossible, to measure with the physical senses. The basic standard to measure the acceptability of the resource material used here is what we call consistency. This means that not only must the subject matter have internal consistency (treated by a single source the same way each time it is dealt with), but it must be treated the same way by at least one other internally consistent source. Additionally, insights into the material presented here from the dreams, meditation experiences, and visions of the author were used. Great care was taken that these personal, intuitive experiences meet the same criteria of internal and external consistency as all other resource material used and that they not be given disproportionate weight because of their personal nature.

We will incorporate a great deal of insights from the work of Edgar Cayce, Rudolf Steiner, Carl Jung, Emanuel Swedenborg, P. D. Ouspensky, Elisabeth Kübler-Ross, Raymond Moody, Harmon Bro, Henry Reed, Mark Thurston, Gershom Scholem, Ken Carey, and others. No body of information had as enormous an influence on each and every chapter of this work as did the more than fourteen thousand psychic discourses of Edgar Cayce. Owing to the difficulty of giving finite explanation to infinite conditions, we will frequently illustrate by comparison.

No work or group of works can outweigh the knowledge gained from a single rich personal experience. It is our hope that this book will supply the tools with which such genuine experience may be understood and effectively used.

Introduction

Contemplating the state we call death arouses varied emotions in all of us at different times. Life and death are our two masters and we do "cling to one and hate the other." Accordingly it is most productive to be absorbed in our choice. It certainly would not be helpful while living in this world to be so absorbed in life in other realms that we couldn't function productively and vice versa. Still if we consider creation as an ongoing experience we should be concerned with that condition we call death, not so much out of fear or longing but to better understand the consistency and continuity of our own being.

In a very general sense we have access to all types of reality all of the time. We receive its impulses but are selective about which part of it we attune to. We do so to preserve a sense of order with which we can work. A helpful illustration would be how a radio operates. The radio receives all transmissions simultaneously, but it would not be very useful if we did not have the ability to listen to one transmission at a time. Consider, would the beauty of Mozart remain so moving if combined with the Boston Pops rendition of the Beatles, while at the same time Bruce Springsteen so eloquently sings of his

America, during which the latest events in the Middle East are being analyzed, against a background of a world series baseball game? This is the least of the confusion that would be caused if a radio could not focus or tune to a single transmission at a time and block out the others. In fact if it couldn't so focus, the radio would be useless, fit only for transmitting noise and confusion. Using this illustration as an analogy, we should appreciate that we have access to much more than we actually transform into conscious awareness. To be helpful, we must have selective separations of the massive amount of details we are receiving so as not to create chaos in our lives. As our understanding of what we perceive grows through our application of it, our awareness of it will increase proportionately.

Paul, the disciple and indefatigable missionary of Christ, said that the view of the spiritual realms from this one could be perceived "as through a glass darkly." Although this illustration had great significance to the Jewish mystic of Tarsus, it often obscures more than it reveals to those of us who try to learn from it two thousand years later. Acknowledging that it is helpful to have an understanding or at least an indication of what lies outside of our day-to-day reality, let us take a look at the clues to what is in the "dark" we fear or embrace so much. To do so we must accept that God is both consistent and lawful, for this approach is the fundamental underpinning to the entirety of all that will follow here.

It is not an inability to see in the dark that obscures the vision of what lies beyond material reality but an unwillingness to see in the light of where we are. Consequently, our vision may benefit all those who occupy this dimension with us. It has been said that we should be no more spiritual than we can manifest in materiality and no more material than we can spiritualize. Certainly we should have no greater clarity of vision of what lies beyond than will make us better equipped to complete the tasks for which we have entered this lifetime.

"It is not all of life to live nor all of death to die," the Edgar Cayce psychic discourses so poetically noted. (900-331) Life is more than we experience in materiality and death is more than leaving this dimension. There are certain consistencies, certain similarities among the varied states that make up the whole of what life really is. The process of trying to understand helps each of us because it gives us an infinitely better understanding of where we are and begins to fasten together the various dimensions of reality in our experience.

Chapter 1

IN THE BEGINNING

BEFORE THE DAWN

Conventional theology holds that there is only one ultimate source of life. All that has ever been or will ever be created is drawn from that source we call God and expressed in an infinite variety of forms. This is the absolute reality in creation—all that can ever be is created by and through our Creator.

Contemporary philosophy instructs us that life does not flow aimlessly but is expressed in an orderly fashion as what we call spirit. It is important to make the distinction that God is not spirit. Spirit is a living portion of God, expressed in a variety of forms and manifest in realms suitable for the unfoldment of each individual expression. In discourse 5749-3, the psychic, Edgar Cayce, notes, "The spirit is the impelling influence of infinity, or the one creative source, force, that is manifest."

Combining the underlying creation philosophy found in the works of Rudolf Steiner and the psychic discourses of Edgar Cayce paints a bold, brilliantly colored picture of creation. In His infinite imagination God imaged life as a microcosm of Himself and expressed this thought in spirit. At its very center was its creative component, that which made it itself. This is what the Cayce discourses call will—not the variety of will we are used to, such as the freedom to choose, for choice is only one expression of will. Based on the Cayce and Steiner philosophies, will is that very center of creation through which life is transformed and brought into all dimensions. Will, therefore, is that which transforms the spirit of God as it re-creates life in all forms. If we follow the pattern of creation found in the Cayce discourses, we find that will acting upon spirit created about itself the body of experience we here call mind. To illustrate the point, one should imagine photons of light flowing in all directions as spirit shining forth from its source. Now we completely surround the light with a thin green glass which we shall call will. The result is a green light glowing outward; this glow we will call the Mind. Everything which is illuminated by this Mind will bear the imprint of the will and appear green. Proceeding with the unfoldment of this pattern, as will acted upon the life it was transforming, the body of experience, the mind, continued to grow around it. This was the beginning of fulfillment, that will acting upon spirit, in accord with the pattern of its creator, built a living, growing expression (mind) with a destiny of its own. It will be helpful as we proceed to note that esoteric teachings equate the spirit with the Heart of God, the will with the Mind of God, and the result, which we have here called mind, as the Word of God.

The Word, as a continuing, growing expression of its Creator, embodies both the spirit which is its life and the will which gives life form. Combining the Cayce philosophy with the Jewish mystical teachings found in the works of the Kabbalah, we see that God took from Himself in this way and expressed life, so it would re-create itself in accord with the perfect pattern of creation which flowed through it. Now here is the pattern of creation, Love expressing love in such a way that it becomes a living re-creation of itself with a life of its own. From the very first, in that movement of God which created will, its ultimate mission was imprinted upon it. So encompassing was this mission that it became both the origin and destiny, the overriding motivation in its creation, according to the Edgar Cayce discourses, that the Word "may know itself to be itself yet one with God." Following the philosophy in the Cayce work, when there had been adequate experience and Mind had grown sufficiently, it divided into infinite parts each a perfect replica of the whole. Each part then contained all of the attributes of the whole, singularly lacking the clarity of the whole but collectively being the whole. Each of the parts had an individuality yet shared a common destiny. Each part had a destiny to build experiences of its own in reality by acting upon life as one with the whole. Each portion of the divided Word now had what could be conceived of as its own mind but better understood as an individually evolving portion of the whole mind. And there we were, individual soul entities each embodying spirit and will within mind—our mind.

It must be noted that as parts of the whole we each had the same origin and destiny, the same mission as the Word. It is worth repeating that mission which is to know ourselves to be ourselves and yet one with our God. Important as this mission is to each and every living soul, it requires further explanation. What *is* knowing ourselves to be ourselves and one with God? How may we come to know ourselves to be individuals yet one with our God? To know one's self to be one's self, one must experience the self as an individual. To know one's self to be one with God, one must experience the varied expressions of God. To combine both as part of a single mission one must experience the varied expressions of God through one's own individuality. In the beginning we were one with God; even when the Christ as the Whole divided, we did not have a sense of self. We had no individual experiences yet; we had not yet gone out into eternity. Even though we were a part of the whole we were unaware of it. Like a newborn baby, we did not yet know where mother left off and baby began. We knew ourselves only as a part of the First Cause, when in fact we were individual parts of the Word, which in turn was an individual part of its Creator. It would yet take eons of experience to gradually awaken us to our individuality and much more to come into a healthy realization of our relationship to the whole. To become aware of our own individuality, we would have to express it. Only experience would build sufficient awareness of ourselves. The more we expressed our individuality the more aware of ourselves we would become. No work more movingly describes in almost poetic terms our state of oneness and subsequent growth as does *Starseed, the Third Millennium*, by Ken Carey. If the Cayce and Steiner works drew a miraculous picture of creation, then Ken Carey surely added the brilliant images.

Likewise, the more of God we experienced, the more we would know our Creator. From the level of will we would make choices. We would not merely decide, but so creatively would we choose that we would build the result into our soul body which is our individual mind. We would act in so creative a fashion that we would have dominion over all that God expressed in spirit. We would be cocreators with our Lord as individuals using eternity and all that was within as our workshop. Everything we would encounter would be an expression of its Lord. As we as individuals would move through creation and experience it as cocreators, we would be experiencing the all of God that is manifest in spirit.

Now we are moving closer to a partial understanding of what it is to experience God through our own individuality. If we were to stop our exploration here, we would have a rather confined and stunted sense of our mission. We are all parts of the whole, created as such and destined to be so. This obviously does not diminish our individuality nor do we lose our identity. Our God does not look upon us with any less favor, nor do we lose our personal relationship with our Lord because we are part of a larger whole. We do not sacrifice individual destiny or uniqueness, but to the contrary, they are enhanced immeasurably. So important is our relationship to the whole and our position in it that we are compelled now to explore this further. Such an understanding can best be gained by illustration. Eastern philosophers have noted that it is not much of an accomplishment for a drop of water to be separated from an ocean, still retaining all of the properties of the larger body, and then at some point be returned to the ocean with a newly acquired self-awareness. The true miracle is that once the drop is removed and its individuality realized, the entire ocean may then be poured into that drop. Once understood, this illustration, although clothed in Eastern mysticism, is a perfect approximation of our position in creation.

We are inseparably connected to all of creation. We are all made of the same stuff, so to speak, and we come from the same place. We are different expressions of the same spirit. We and our fellow souls that make up the Word, which Edgar Cayce also called the Christ Consciousness, are inseparable. We are joined together in origin, mission, and destiny. The same life flows through each of us, and our very being is held in place by its relationship to all of the members of the whole. We are also joined together with all of the members of the Word in our consciousness of reality. None of us therefore can experience anything that ultimately does not affect all of the others. As we all grow in individuality we all benefit from the experience of one another. We lose nothing here but quite the opposite, we benefit incalculably by such a connectedness to each other. Whether we term such connectedness the Collective Unconscious, as did Carl Jung, or the Christ Consciousness, as did Edgar Cayce, it is nonetheless the pool of awareness to which, and from which, each of us adds and every soul draws. The results of all soul experiences find their home in the Word. Each and every soul is destined to embody the Word we call Christ. As we grow in experience, in keeping with the pattern imprinted within spirit by our God, we become better enabled to embody and express more of the Whole. In so doing we ultimately become one with the Whole, and the ocean is poured into the individual drop of water.

Now that we have drawn a clear picture of our relationship with reality and connectedness with one another, we must add depth to the images so they will not remain two dimensional. We have placed all of the images in the picture, and now we need to focus on ourselves there to understand better what we see. What are we to the whole? A cell? A limb? An organ? We are an exact replica of the whole with all of its attributes but alone we are lacking in clarity. Henry Reed in his book, *Awakening Your Psychic Powers,* uses the term "holographic soul," and views the soul's position in this regard. So astute is his observation that it bears further discussion.

Normally an object is seen in three dimensions because it reflects light in all directions around it. The reflections interact to give the quality of light, shade, and depth. A conventional camera cannot capture all of this but is limited to light and shades, while holography adds depth by measuring the distance the light has traveled as well. The laser makes possible holographic imagery as never before available. The result of this technology is to produce a light which Reed terms "coherent," a straight beam made up of photons all on the same wavelength and all striking the object at exactly the same time. When the laser beam is split, part of it lights up the object and is reflected onto a treated plate. The other part of the beam is reflected directly into the plate and the two beams combine to make an impression on the plate. When a laser light of the same intensity is shone through the plate at the same angle but in the opposite direction, a three-dimensional image is projected, seemingly hanging in the air. Now, if we were to inspect the holographic negative, we would not see the reverse pattern of the object which is being produced, as on a conventional negative. We would in fact not see anything which makes sense to us; we would see swirls of photo impressions on the negative. At this point imagine breaking the plate into many small pieces. If we retrieve one piece and shine through it a laser of the same intensity that produced it in the opposite direction as originally shone, we would not see just a part of the original image but the whole image: the object in its entirety. The same result would take place no matter which of the many pieces were retrieved. No part of the original image would be lacking except for its sharpness. The more pieces added, the clearer the image would become. All of the image is impressed on each and every piece of the plate. No piece of the plate, no matter how small or large has more or less of the image. Each has imprinted the image of the whole upon it from an ever so slightly different angle, together reflecting the whole from all angles. Through this illustration we have a better understanding of our relationship to the whole. For most of us this additional perspective can and should evolve into an understanding of much more than just ourselves.

At the center of the individual mind there are the will and the spirit. Collectively these three divisions (spirit, will, and mind) have come to be known as the soul. As the mind grows, there develop many levels, for mind is not one mass of experience but layer upon layer, line upon line of experience. The Cayce discourses often state that imprinted upon each soul is the pattern of creation, and toward its center is an awareness of being eternal.

It is well here to question how differences resulted, following the division of the Word. As each of the newly formed parts of the whole evolved, they began to become aware of themselves. As such a gradual awakening took place in each soul, so too did the awareness of its proximity to the Source. All radios, no matter how similar in structure, have a reception different from each other, owing to the somewhat different angle in relation to the transmission. So too does each and every soul, by virtue of its relative position to the Source of Life. It is from this difference that each soul grows in the direction of that uniqueness, and develops an individuality different from any other soul.

The soul, the eternal component of each and every one of us, is the storehouse of all experience. As it is not bound by time and space, the soul has access to all it has experienced as well as to the experiences of all others. In his book, *Theosophy,* Rudolf Steiner wrote, "The soul is the connecting link between the spirit of man and his body. Its forces of sympathy and antipathy that, owing to their mutual relationship, bring about soul manifestations such as desire, sensitivity, wish, thinking and aversion." Creative in essence, the soul is the origin of thought, desire, sensitivity, hope, fantasy, and fear. Difficult as it may be at this point to accept, the eternal soul, not the corporal body, is the focal point of emotions, imagination, creativity, and all that is related to them. It is the depository of all it has actively experienced and all it has been taken through. No experience is lost and everything has constructive potential. Out of this well of eternity we call our soul rises all of the creativity we are likely to encounter, physically, mentally, and spiritually.

MORNING

We return to Ken Carey's moving creation images in *Starseed, the Third Millennium* and carry them yet another step in their unfoldment. To do this we mix in some Cayce, some Steiner, and a generous helping of Jewish mysticism. In the timeless, spaceless expanse of eternity, God's Thought was expressed. It could not be seen or heard, nor was it perceptible to that spiritual dimension for which it was destined. It was as invisible to the senses of the spiritual realm as our thoughts are to the material dimension. Life was expressed in spirit and in this living thought God imaged the entirety of the third-dimensional reality. God's thought contained the patterns of reality, the creative elements of will, the universe in all of its glory and the image of time and space in which it would all unfold. It drew to itself that of which this spiritual realm consisted, acted upon spirit, transformed it, and built about itself a boundless spiritual body. Its nucleus was not spirit, but its outer layers which it produced from the substance of the spiritual realm were. At first, as the process began it was barely recognizable to the spiritual dimension, perceptible more as a presence than as an image. Then, this thought, embraced by spirit, began to glow, first unnoticeably and then it became brighter. As it drew more and more spirit to itself, it seemed to grow in intensity, in size, and "then there was light." It was the mind of God acting on spirit, a beginning in reality.

When it was ripe, when it had gathered sufficient of the realm of spirit, all at once it exploded. At its very center was love's need to express itself. It flew out in all directions at once, like love exploding from the heart in search of its own. It was not a random explosion, not a

disconnected flying apart but was more like a macro-
cosmic inflation. It flew across the face of infinity and
filled reality, as light fills the darkness. It replaced nothing but illuminated everything. Within its expanse, there
it was—time and space—a new dimension in a universe
of dimensions, expanding across eternity, a new expression of its creator. This new realm expanded like an endless balloon while an entire consciousness was exploding
into reality and pushing out its borders in every direction. Then, from the center came forth that substance
from which the universe would evolve, filling time and
space with energy on an unimaginable scale. Now this
energy which filled space appeared almost as a distortion against the blackness of its background. Within the
embrace of this energy, flying endlessly from the center,
evolved the gases congealing around points of consciousness, which began to take on visible image. Finally
there it was; matter, energy slowed to its lowest rate of
vibration, with the gases held together by consciousness
crystallized into a universe of matter. All of this was in
motion, time, space, energy, and matter—moving out
from the center from which endless creation continued
to expand in all directions.

The process is continuous, since time and space continue to expand through reality and materiality fills it as
quickly as it expands. From the very center of this dimension is a love that cannot be contained in itself and
a creative will that cannot lie dormant. It must expand,
it must express, it must create, and here is where we find
our home—inside of the thought of God.

Let us take a closer look at time and space, this unique
dimension in a universe of dimensions. We have named
it materiality, after the lowest common denominator
within the realm. Difficult as it is to grasp, there is nowhere else in all of reality where time and space exist as
expressions of their Creator. Edgar Cayce described the

three dimensions of our earthly reality as time, space, and patience.

In discourse 451-3 Cayce noted that one may express patience by "becoming aware of that which is the impelling influence in thine experience." Patience then is that impelling force in creation which ultimately draws all expressions of life into conformity with that from which it was formed. Life is manifest in every level of reality from its most primal expression to its least. In *Heaven and Its Wonders and Hell from Things Heard and Seen,* the mystic Emanuel Swedenborg notes that "nothing can spring from itself, but only from something prior to itself." Certainly, all expressions of life in the earth are manifestations of a more primal form expressed in higher realms. Like an onion, each outer layer holds the shape of that layer which immediately preceded it. Unlike the onion and all of nature around us, we can resist conformity to that from which we are formed for an indefinite period. But we cannot do this permanently. Patience is not a passive force, it is not a waiting. Patience is a persistence to conform to that more primal life of which we are made. Patience is never bold, never inconsistent, and never neglectful. Patience is always gentle, always even, and always at work. In materiality, patience is that which makes it possible for all life to be bound to all it expresses and to grow as the reflection of that which it embodies. For all souls, the dimension of patience in materiality allows us to persist in dealing with those obstacles we have placed between ourselves and our destiny. As a direct result of patience we are inevitably drawn toward conformity with the higher forms of life we embody. Essentially, patience is that which impels us toward perfection, or it allows us to withdraw from life in the earth and take up the challenge another day.

Space, Cayce notes, is the dimension in which we create the illusion of separateness, not only from our Cre-

ator but from each other. This appearance of separation
allows us to measure progress; it yields the concept of
distance. Space is a measuring device by which we may
evaluate movement. The Cayce discourses further noted
that time allows us to measure our movement on a
gradual basis. It gives us the luxury of a gradual movement rather than meeting everything at once. It is not as
difficult as one might imagine to conceive of an awareness in which less emphasis is placed on time and space.
We need only to go back a few hours to when we were
asleep and dreaming. Perhaps we had a mix of charac-
ters and situations from different times in our life, all in-
teracting within the same time. Perhaps we were in one
place and suddenly found ourselves in another. At times
we view ourselves from a distance, as in the third person, and yet at times we view ourselves from the inside
out. These are very common occurrences in dreams, and
clearly overcome the fetters of time and space. The odd
part is that while in that realm we think all of this quite
natural, and it is not until we awake and reinvest our
awareness in time and space that the occurrences from
the night before seem unusual. If we could in fact record
our dreams and develop a working relationship with
them, we would have a better understanding of reality
as it exists beyond materiality. Rudolf Steiner and Edgar
Cayce were among those who observed that the dream
state was more reality than illusion and that it was akin
to those dimensions we experience after physical death.

So that we do not lose accuracy for simplicity's sake, it
must now be noted that materiality is not one dimension but many. The material dimensions are tied closely
to one another, and each successive realm reaches further out from the center. As we move outward through
these realms, the laws which keep order in physical reality gradually become of less effect. So gradual is the
movement between the realms of materiality, so broad

is the overlapping of conditions, that we most often overlook the divisions if we are not looking very carefully for them. It may be a long leap between the realms in which we dream and those in which we are awake, but how close are we to the reality of our own imagination. How fine is the line between imagination and application, and when do we become aware that we have left the domain of one and entered the reality of the other? Life is full of examples of how movement is gradual. In fact the lawfulness of this pattern of natural progression permeates all realms of materiality.

Here we have the workshop in which we find ourselves, body, mind, and soul. We are blessed with the ability that through application we may become one with and ultimately rule, as cocreators, the entire material realm with all that it contains.

WATCHMEN

We find in the Cayce discourses several references to our participating in creation. We were not only witnesses to the creation of materiality but we were participants in the process. As one with the whole, not yet separating ourselves in consciousness from it, we were an integral part of all that went into the creation of the physical realms. We beheld the creative seed from which would unfold the entire universe in all of its glory. We watched as all of the laws poured out into reality through which an entire dimension would find expression. In touch with all creation that we held together, we became, with the angelic ministers of grace, points of transformation. As focal points of transformation, we acted upon spirit in such a way that it was converted into matter. How it would unfold and the form it would take were imprinted as a pattern within the very seed from which materiality sprang. As the pattern of the entire tree lies within the apple seed, so too does the pattern for materiality lie within the seed of the physical realm. Emanuel Swedenborg as well as Rudolf Steiner described what we here call seeds as germs or germ points in creation. Swedenborg had incredibly detailed visions, and he wrote eloquent descriptions of how germ points operate.

According to the Cayce information, we were here fulfilling our purpose as cocreators, one with our God yet as individuals. Edgar Cayce insisted that nothing would exist in the entire universe that was not somewhere within each of us. Once complete, the entire dimension would bear our fingerprints. We would be an integral part of it and it of us. Then somewhere along the way some of us turned in the wrong direction. We deviated from the pattern, at first ever so slightly. In time we moved further and further from its path. Like two lines on a parallel course, one beginning to move at a slightly different angle from the other, the longer they become the farther apart they will grow. Ken Carey beautifully described our movement which corresponds so well to the information found in the Edgar Cayce discourses. We became excited with the individual aspects of our being and what was resulting. This, in and of itself, was not outside of God's original plan for each soul. But we moved further into our own individualities than we were prepared lawfully to express toward the rest of creation. We were to move no further into individuality than we were prepared to express what we found as one with the whole. Likewise, we were to move no further into spirituality than we were prepared to materialize. In excessive attention to the whole we lose awareness of our individuality and in allowing ourselves to become too involved in our individuality we lose sight of our relationship with the whole. Like a pendulum, the balanced movement from one side to the other is vital to its designed operation. Here is where our difficulties began. It was not the awareness of ourselves that began what we call the "fall," but it came about as the result of a disproportionate awareness of ourselves. We were ready for such awareness but we, through our own choice, were unwilling to express it properly. Instead of choosing to express what we were experiencing, we chose to become those experiences. A vital part of our mission was to creatively add to the whole, but we chose instead to add to ourselves.

Not all of us began self-preoccupation at the same point, nor is it possible to estimate how many did. At best we could guess that only a small portion of all the souls created began to turn toward themselves.

Edgar Cayce noted that all of creation looked upon this in horror as we began our "fall." As we moved further and further from the oneness we were created to inhabit, we built about ourselves a crust-like body which further separated us from the whole. Gradually our light grew dimmer and we became less and less aware of our heritage. There is no way to measure the length of time over which this transformation took place, because time as we know it did not exist. This was occurring in realms where reality was not measurable by such standards. The Cayce scenario indicates that, try as they could, there was no way our fellow souls, the angelic ministry, or any other part of creation could stop or even slow the sequence of events taking place. At the very center of our being was our will, that which made us ourselves; freedom to choose is a quality of will. It was totally opposed to God's plan that any part of creation take from created souls any aspect of our will. To entertain the desire to interfere with our expression of will, no matter how misguided the expression, would be to compound the fall from oneness. The "fall" was not limited to souls, members of the Word, but included inhabitants of the angelic kingdom as well. It was chaos spread across perfection and no one knew where it would end.

As we moved through creation, in the dimness of our vision, we began to experience the forming material dimension. We began to mix with the patterns within the very seed from which they would flower. Gradually we began to change the forces which would eventually form time and space and ultimately to interfere with all of those forces which would eventually form this material realm. At this point a more perfect part of creation, including angels, souls, and those appointed the tasks of assisting the unfolding of creation, moved in awareness into the forming physical realms. According to the discourses of Edgar Cayce, they "came together to reason in the elements" and by force of their perfection healed those forces which by now had been perverted. (137-4) They brought to bear the full force of love and grace by which they converted and restored the forces of life taking shape in materiality. Once the manifesting life force was restored and conformed to the original pattern within it, those who had come to help brought into this dimension laws which would assist in our eventual healing and return to oneness. Patterns were manifest by them which would inevitably draw all who would come to properly express them back to the state they enjoyed before the "fall." These new manifestations would eventually come to be known as universal laws. They are those by which we may express infinite patterns in finite reality. Cayce said that all of creation sang with joy that God's plan was expressed and we would not be irretrievably lost.

Here in creation is where we would begin our journey back to that state we held in oneness. Here is where we would have countless opportunities to return balance to our souls. Here in time, space, and patience within the laws of materiality we would find our real selves. Here we would have this unique opportunity to work with the law of cause and effect in the only part of creation where it rules supreme. For it is not from justice or fairness this realm was propelled but from the universal law of cause and effect. There would be no activity within this dimension, save God's grace, that would escape compliance with cause and effect.

We must point out that at this time our destiny was not to walk the earth and eat of its bounty. We were to inhabit those other realms of materiality surrounding the earth and to walk the earth when appropriate more in spirit than as hardened matter. The Cayce creation story implies that we were not meant to participate in this realm so deeply that the consciousness necessary to inhabit material form would make us spiritually myopic. Cause and effect, which we were meant to grow through, operate on other material levels surrounding hardened matter. This however was not to be our own chosen workshop.

Lower and lower we went into the realms of materiality. We watched from the inside out as matter took on form. We mixed with the patterns, we copied them, we created forms of our own and inhabited those forms. So complete was our mischievous bent that we began to invest creative aspects of our consciousness not only in the hardened forms that we found lawfully unfolding, but also in those we ourselves created. As creative beings, we acted upon matter in such a fashion as to transform it by force of our imagination. The more involved we became in matter, the more we lost sight of our immortality. We became trapped, forgetting from where we came and ultimately the way back. As we became so overwhelmingly conscious of ourselves, the loss of consciousness of our God resulted in the realization of mortality. Now began the age of fear and the beginning of our need to dominate all expressions of life. For if we were indeed mortal, then others could destroy us. Faith was replaced by fear and love by indifference. As we blocked out the qualities we had embodied in spirit the void left was quickly filled by the chaos which resulted.

As we are addressing the transformation of the spirit of love into the spirit of confusion we must now deviate somewhat to explain the Satanic manifestation. When one reads Emanuel Swedenborg's perspective on Satan, it may at first seem more confusing than educational. He states that Satan is evil only in materiality and that outside of material influence Satan has never been corrupted. He notes that the Satanic forces are destructive only when they enter the material realms but are constructive elsewhere. Such a notion shocks the sensitivity of Western thought where Satan is considered the spiritual embodiment of evil. We most often think of Satan as the angel cast out of the presence of God, confined to the lower depths of reality.

The Cayce material described Satan not as a being but as a collective negativity. It is that pool of negativity into which every evil adds to its volume and upon which we may draw at will. Incorporating these perspectives, we can see the Satanic forces as something aside from inherently evil. This is by no means to view them as wholesome, for they are truly deviant and pull upon the very fabric of our salvation. For accuracy's sake, though, it must be noted that the points of consciousness from which flows the formation of spirit into matter have been so assaulted by our unlawful influence that part of what they manifest is negative. It is in these crossroads of life which we call points of consciousness that we have stored our collective selfishness. Evil draws its creativity in the earth from here. All that manifests passes through both positive and negative patterns. The results of our misguided activities transform the life which passes through it, and these negative patterns are the Satanic forces in action. Further, it is appropriate to mention the

Prince of Darkness whom we call Lucifer. Lucifer was an archangel who fell from grace leading a portion of the angelic kingdom into darkness. The same angel is named Sammael (the Prince of Demons) in the Jewish mystical works of the Kabbalah. Sammael translated into English is Satan; thus the confusion. Because we will from time to time refer to Satanic forces, they were introduced here. The Luciferian influence will not be a point of discussion but was mentioned briefly to clarify its relationship to the Satanic forces.

Our initial experience in hardened matter was exciting. Then as our awareness dimmed, great fear set in. We now found ourselves trapped, unable to get back to where we began. After a time others came to help us. Some became trapped like ourselves and some did not. So horrible was our plight that our God intervened on our behalf. Cayce noted that with a soul in perfection God reasoned our rescue. All of creation grew according to patterns which permeated reality. Form, in whatever dimension it resided, will inevitably and inescapably be drawn into the pattern of perfection through which it was expressed. The pattern for the salvation of our souls needed to be set where we were in materiality; this was the opportunity to do so. This task, being accomplished, would be more than just a mold; it would be the pattern, the path, the way to which every living soul would eventually be drawn into escape. Now the stage was set and we began our long and often painful journey Home.

LOGOS

The Soul which reasoned with God, creating the plan for the salvation of its fellow souls, became incarnate as part of this plan. This Soul did not at first incarnate in skin and bone as we would imagine but in a much finer substance. For proper identity we will here call this sav-

ior the Master Soul. The Cayce discourses have quite a
bit to say about this Master Soul as well as its journey.
Much of the story is brought together well by Glenn
Sanderfur in his *Lives of the Master: The Rest of the Jesus
Story.* There was no need at this point for the Master Soul
to be so deeply immersed in materiality as to wear a
body made up of the physical elements of the earth. This
Soul drew to It the elements surrounding the earth from
which matter was forming and put on a less confining,
much more versatile, finer body. It was material but a
less dense material than that of which the earth would
ultimately be composed. It was necessary to keep so
close a connection with the spiritual realms that any
deeper immersion into materiality would have made
such an association impossible. In this state of being,
this Soul, the Master Soul, would transform spirit to
make manifest in the types, archetypes, and laws that
which was needed for the salvation of the souls trapped
in the earth. Creation as an ongoing process continued;
the number of us confined in matter continued to increase. Drawing upon the Word, this Master Soul was
totally creative and had no limits to what It could do.

Dominion over the entire material dimension and all
that it contained was vested in this Being. It would bring
into reality all of the laws now necessary to complete the
mission It assumed. The Soul itself became the pattern
of physical perfection to which all souls would ultimately be drawn. Escape from confinement in materiality would only be possible by conformity to the pattern
being manifested by the Master Soul. The pattern would
ultimately become known as "the Way" in Judeo-Christian theology. The draw to Its perfection was so strong
that neither time nor space would diminish its magne-
tism in any way. The attraction was irresistible, and conformity was only a matter of time. The Cayce material
indicates that Archangel Michael was given charge pro-

tecting this pattern manifested for the souls' return to perfection—Michael thus becoming the Lord of the Way. Once the attention was changed in each of us and our focus was less on ourselves, the magnetic draw and conformity to perfection were inevitable. New forces were set in motion to allow for this while at the same time this Master Soul began healing those other forces which had been perverted by our preoccupation with ourselves in the earth.

There were those powers which arose to combat the effort to free all of us, in fear that they would perish, for it was mortality and not immortality that was the watchword of the time. Countless ministers of grace assisted in this new dawn. The combat between the forces of light and darkness (which has not ended) began in the elements surrounding the earth, not as a personal confrontation but by force of their respective influences. The darker forces held to fear and selfishness while the forces of light held to love and faith. The dark cannot exist where there is light unless those who carry the light are willing to extinguish it. No darkness, no matter how much the volume, can put out a light, no matter how little the quantity. It should be understood that light, spiritual light, is the reflection of life lawfully manifested, while darkness is the absence of such a presence. Simply stated, light, physically and spiritually, is a thing while darkness is the lack of a thing. Likewise, the forces of good are a lawful expression of life, while the forces of evil are the absence of such expression.

From this vantage point the Master Soul was able to work with the germ points of materiality, as well as the forms in which they were expressed, in the realms surrounding the physical earth. Thus the work, God's work, was carried out. Through the Cayce perspective we see that as the work progressed the time once again became right for division. Following the pattern of creation, imprinted within the Word, it was good that the Master Soul express itself by division. (Glenn Sanderfur did an excellent job excerpting from the Cayce discourses here.) This naturally resulted in a procreation of itself. This was accomplished by what appeared to be the dividing of the Soul's spirit forces from Its will forces. In actuality certain forces in each would be accentuated and others suppressed. The "positive" portion of the division magnified that part of the soul which was involved in amplifying life. Not as one might think, as in creating life, but by being a focal point, by drawing upon a portion of energy and amplifying it. The "positive" soul thus took upon itself a relationship with the whole that was based upon amplifying spirit that all it touched might live. The "negative" soul, which amplified the will forces, became the transformer of spirit and gave form to life in whatever realm of reality it chose. One can only assume such a division was necessary for the unfoldment of God's plan and that it no doubt followed the pattern of procreation set in motion eons earlier. We have come to call the positive and negative forces masculine and feminine. Let us here look back to the holographic concept, that in which each soul had imprinted upon it the pattern of the entire Master Soul. Alone, each presented a less clear image of the Soul from which they came but together the clarity of the Master Soul was perfect. The suppression of certain gifts allowed for the focusing of attention on the remaining ones. So the two, now male and female, began their work together in perfect unity.

In the earth fear and selfishness were stirred up by the agony of separation, and they were spreading on a massive scale. As the situation grew worse the focus of attention of the master souls needed to become narrower and narrower. As a result they moved closer and closer in consciousness to materiality. So close was their attention that they were often visible to the inhabitants of the earth. To those of us who beheld them, they would have appeared at times to fade in and out of sight. At such times they were visible although not solid. Such a proximity was necessary in order to work with the souls in torment and to manifest the pattern for salvation in the material realms closest to the earth. We find reference in the Edgar Cayce discourses that this period lasted some two hundred thousand years. (364-4) As the work was completed in the realms surrounding the earth, few if any of the souls would allow themselves to rise from the depths even to become aware of what had been done. They were immersed in such darkness that the light would have to be brought to them in the lowest levels of materiality. Now the work which the patterns, the master souls, completed in the higher realms of materiality would have to be expressed by them in the lower ones.

Nowhere in materiality was there a form made from the substance of the earth which was suitable for such a work. The vehicle for the soul in the earth would have to be of such a nature that it acted perfectly with material laws in the earth and at the same time did not in any way inhibit complete spiritual awareness. The angelic host, souls, and the Spiritual Forces came together with the master souls to create such a vehicle. When complete, the body, mind, and soul of the male manifestation of the Master Soul was poured into the material body they had fashioned. The work continued for a while as the way was prepared for the movement into matter of the female manifestation. Then, the process again began, following the pattern of division already set in motion. Material forces from the male were drawn off to prepare the vehicle for the female—the male again generating the life force, the female transforming it, and then each occupying the result. For those interested in elapsed time, the Cayce discourses once noted a period of about forty years over which this process, the creation of the female vehicle, took place. There is no way of knowing if Cayce was giving this period as actual elapsed time or as a symbolic period. There they were, the father and mother of us all, Adam and Eve. Their chosen task was to now work from the inside out, to build the road which led from the depths of materiality to the heights of spirituality. They chose to make manifest the Word in material form and to make of themselves that road by which we would all travel home.

Chapter 2

LIFE IN THE EARTH

BODY, MIND, AND SOUL

Until now we have spoken of ourselves as Spirit, Will, Mind, and Body. Essentially they are all one but it is helpful to keep a three-dimensional perspective in the earth. Mark Thurston, keenly aware of this, once commented that his outer skin was the edge of his soul. For the sake of clarity it should be repeated that spirit is the impelling force of life, flowing from our God and expressed in spirituality. Will is the creative point in each of us through which spirit passes. Mind is the result of will acting upon spirit and the physical is what is built in materiality by mind acting upon spirit. As stated earlier, Edgar Cayce often said, "The spirit is life; the mind is the builder; the physical is the result." (349-4) The so-called soul is a combination of these forces. One can take Thurston's insightful approach and say the physical is the outer crust of the soul or take a more conservative approach and stop just short of this. For the sake of simplicity we will lean more toward the concepts of Emanuel Swedenborg and define the boundaries of the soul as including spirit, will, and mind, but the physical as well as its consciousness will be the result of the soul acting upon materiality.

Thomson Jay Hudson, in *The Law of Psychic Phenomena,* illustrated that our mind, with its many levels, is the only part of us resident in the spiritual and material dimensions at the same time. This was not a new concept, even in Hudson's time, but his approach was. An attorney, editor, and scholar, Hudson had a methodical approach, meticulous research, and a highly objective perspective. His approach was scientific and scholarly. Let us now take a closer look at the mind from a time and space perspective. The Edgar Cayce discourses on mind note, " . . . the earthly or material consciousness is ever tempered with material combinations; the superconsciousness with the consciousness between soul and spirit, and partakes of the spiritual forces principally. In consciousness we find only projections of subconscious and superconscious, which conditions project themselves in dreams, visions, unless entered into the superconscious forces. In the consciousness of earthly or material forces there enters all the attributes of the physical, fleshly body. In the subconscious there enters the attributes of soul forces, and of the conscious forces. In the superconscious there enters the subconscious forces, and spiritual discernment and development." (900-16) Here we have a perspective of mind expressed in three distinct parts. The superconscious is the soul mind. It is that mind formed by the will acting upon spirit. The subconscious is that portion of mind formed by the superconscious acting upon spirit. The conscious mind is formed by the result of the subconscious acting upon spirit. As life moves outward in our being we have the opportunity to act upon it at each level so that we may add new aspects to ourselves.

One might think that as we act upon life it moves only outward from ourselves. It is important to take note that no activity we can produce can escape its ultimate destiny of being assimilated as part of us. Each of our experiences is digested by us and becomes a part of the one or more levels of the body that we call our mind. Each part of the mind is made of the substance of that dimension in which it was formed, and all parts are resident by force of the influence in a living human body. The mind is not the brain, which is used by the mind, but as the reader can see, it is infinitely more. Each portion of our mind is continually growing and being developed. In the earth we are aware largely of our conscious mind and only vaguely aware of the pulls of the subconscious upon it. Outside of this earth it is the subconscious which becomes our fully operative awareness and subject to the influences of the superconscious. The Cayce material further notes that the superconscious in turn becomes the soul mind or the active consciousness in eternity. We are much closer at this point to seeing the entirety of the soul.

We should be aware that the body is not a permanent part of the soul. But also we need to take cognizance that the conscious mind as well as the subconscious mind will take leave of our being eventually. The loss of any part of us will be of little consequence to our eternal being, as that which passed through it will ultimately and permanently be stored in the superconscious.

Let us look a bit closer at the superconscious. Cayce and Steiner agree that it beholds the face of God always and remains uncorrupted. The superconscious mind is in constant touch with all reality and the consciousness therein. It is the part of us from which springs precognition, retrocognition, and prophecy. It is essentially psychic (of the soul) and in touch with past, present, and future all at the same time. It resides in all dimensions as it manifests through appropriate vehicles but has its home only in the most primal. It is through this self, our mind, that the impelling influence of creation is impressed upon the rest of our being. Experiences and their lessons are not lost. The prize whose loss we fear above all else, our identity, is eternal and remains forever with us.

We can approach the mind from the scientific perspective or from an esoteric one, but we will hardly begin our journey when we encounter the vast unknown. Science is continuously revising its theories regarding the nature of our mind. Gaining a better understanding here is much like building a ship in the dark; one cannot see what one is doing and must rely upon senses not customarily used in this task. Even when we do something correctly we cannot see it to verify its correctness. When we stand something upon what has already been built, we cannot step back and see if it is properly in place. When we complete such a seemingly impossible task, we can only hope it will float. How will we know if the understanding we have built will float? Firstly, it will ring true to us; it will fit well. Next, it will be consistent with things we already know. Lastly, we will be able to measure it against things that others know. Unless our perspective is so revolutionary that it springs full grown into life, it should meet the three requisites set forth here.

The subconscious, as we have noted, is that portion of the mind formed by the superconscious acting upon spirit. Quite simply it is the result of what the superconscious has done with life. The subconscious forms about the superconscious like a body, housing it and expressing it in lower dimensions. Cayce noted that the subconscious is made up of experience and built of the finer materials of the realms in which those experiences were obtained. Absolutely nothing is experienced by any of us in materiality that has not first passed through the subconscious. Reality as we know it is projected like a light by the superconscious onto the subconscious. It is the activity in the subconscious that acts like a negative, and what we perceive in the physical as reality is the projection of that subconscious activity upon the face of materiality. We would note here that if we wish to change what we see in reality, we cannot do so by adjusting the image; we must change the subconscious activity being imaged.

At the very edge of the subconscious, surrounding it on all sides, is an energy field we will call the emotional. All that passes in or out of the subconscious must pass through this field. The emotional is not in this position by accident but perfectly placed to act as the springboard for the subconscious. The emotional accelerates our sense of reality so that it moves more smoothly, as it is assimilated by other levels of our mind. In a very rough sense, the emotional field acts as that which gives an extra push to reality, as it passes in and out of the subconscious. As this occurs it stirs what lies within the subconscious, and depending upon what is activated, an emotional response will result. The emotions or what we commonly call feelings are not the emotional as described here, but they are a response to its quickening. We give great weight to our feelings without sufficient understanding that they are not us, but how we feel about us. Without our emotions we would have little useful insight into ourselves. Consequently, without our emotions it is not likely we would be able to fulfill our creative destiny in materiality.

Edgar Cayce noted of the subconscious: " . . . when we speak of subconscious forces and universal forces we are speaking of one and the same." (900-359) While the conscious mind reasons by comparison, the subconscious operates by inductive reasoning. The subconscious is creative in essence and the focal point in materiality from which flows creativity. When we say creativity here, we mean not merely originality but creativity in the broadest possible sense of the word. All knowledge, all that we have experienced in the earth, all that we have

experienced in the interbetween, all that we have experienced in all of the dimensions surrounding materiality
are stored in the subconscious. Likewise, all of the experiences of humankind, from the very beginning, are accessible to the subconscious from the superconscious.
Whereas our superconscious is in touch with collective
consciousness, our subconscious has direct access to
the superconscious part of ourselves. As we in material
consciousness do continuously draw from the subconscious, so too does the subconscious draw from the
superconscious. So fine is the line between conscious
and subconscious, yet it is finer still between the subconscious and superconscious.

Let us here and now make this all personal. When you
had your last thought, where did it come from? Have you
made a wish recently? Have you imagined what could
be? Have you exercised any artistic ability, solved any
difficult problem, had a dream, or been in any way intuitive? Do you have fears, likes, dislikes; have you acted on
faith? These are all expressions of the subconscious and
originate in that portion of our mind. Think of it; so
much of our waking hours is spent acting consciously
upon what flows through from the subconscious, for in
so doing we give material expression to our mental self.
To those of us who explore the origin and destiny of our
own creativity, it is only the most egocentric who would
attribute their motivation to the conscious mind.

Again, the pattern of expression is always the same.
Higher activity is expressed in lower realms to allow for a
more confined focus upon the activity. The superconscious manifests in less primal realms as the subconscious and is expressed in yet even more primal
dimensions as the conscious mind. The higher expression is constantly seeking a more focused expression in
the lower.

If such a focus is hard to imagine let us again illustrate.

Imagine yourself building a bookcase. You think the project will hold all of the books you so love—a place where you will store that which gives you knowledge and enjoyment. You will put into the building process an effort worthy of that which you wish to store. The bookcase will be comparable in quality to its contents. Suddenly the hammer strikes your finger with full force and causes a great deal of pain. For a while at least, your consciousness is drawn from the realms of wisdom, beauty, and knowledge to your finger. You are now totally occupied with the physical pain you feel; all you are, as far as your awareness extends, is a finger and you hurt. To the degree that you have learned that you were not paying enough attention to the materialization of your thoughts in a physical world, you have learned something by the experience. You would have gained a painful lesson but one worth learning. If we wish to make manifest the beauty we image in our minds, we must give it equal energy and focus in materiality, or we may find that materiality exacts our focus in spite of us. If we take this to its constructive conclusion, we will then concentrate on the material project and be motivated by thoughts which have not yet been materially applied. There are many more examples which could be given to illustrate the pattern of focus and application, but they would not have greater credence because of their quantity.

As we move from higher to lower levels of consciousness for the benefit of focus, it is easy to see how we lose sight of where we came from. This forgetfulness is not the way it was meant to be but is a consequence of our struggle. We do not have to recall all that the higher levels of ourselves have experienced. We must however try to awaken the best in ourselves and allow it to influence our lives. This indeed is the job of the subconscious, as it uses the conscious mind and body as the intermediary in this quest. We tend to think of the subconscious as a puff of smoke or an invisible force. The subconscious, Cayce noted, is in fact a body, in which resides our superconscious in finer realms of reality. On those levels we now have the subconscious in "visible" form. To the senses of the finer realms the mind is fully manifest and in fact made up in part of the substance of that reality.

What may our mind look like? It looks strikingly like us. For the answer let us return to the patterns we spoke of. As we manifest outward from spirit, we conform the reality of each dimension to our own images. From each and every level on which we manifest, we draw the substance of which that dimension is comprised, like a magnet. This substance is drawn to us forming the texture of our image appropriate to that dimension. We would not necessarily have skin on another plane but we surely would have an envelope which surrounds us. Picture, if you will, water which has been shaped in a perfect circle. If we pour flour into this water the substance would likewise take on the same shape, and if we solidified it by adding glue the result would take on the shape of the flour which took on the shape of the water. It is important to understand this concept because there is no better example of how patterns manifest throughout reality. They do not change, but the substance they draw to themselves most certainly does.

In other realms this subconscious is called the "astral body" and is perceived to have definite form. There is almost nothing within us that we know in materiality that is absent from the subconscious. As we move further into the astral planes the first thing we would begin to notice as missing are concerns with being mortal or what we term the survival instinct. Next we would notice we are losing all of those emotions connected with this concern for our own mortality. Such a loss does not result in any sort of instant awakening; it all seems quite natural and unemotional. This new condition is quite appropriate. If not being looked for, it just comes upon us both gradually and unnoticed. This is the body described as a "ghost" or a "spirit form." We have all encountered such forms many times in our dreams; they are no less real just because we no longer see them after having moved in consciousness to awaken. In the dream state "ghosts" are not frightening but are so appropriate to the subconscious dreaming mind they are accepted as reality. It is only in the waking state that "spirit forms" seem inappropriate, and we begin to question the quality of our subconscious perceptions. In our waking state we respond more to the influence of our subconscious than we can fully appreciate, as it seeks expression through the conscious mind. In fact our subconscious often reacts to the subconscious of others and this mostly goes unrecognized as well. The potency and dominance of the subconscious is vastly underrated by most of us.

As previously noted, the conscious mind does not reside in the brain. It however uses the brain, as the Cayce discourses noted, as it does the whole of the central nervous system, to express the subconscious in materiality. The central nervous system is the conductor of mental impulse, and its crowning glory in materiality is the brain. As we have pointed out earlier in this chapter, the conscious mind operates by comparative reasoning. It relates current activity to what is stored in the subconscious, as well as past experiences to the external things currently perceived by us. Material consciousness works in very close concert to the five senses and derives its gratification or revulsion from them. The conscious mind is as mortal as is the body and does not survive it. The conscious draws its life from the subconscious acting upon spirit in bodily manifestation. It comes into existence at physical birth and grows throughout a material experience. The conscious mind has no need of surviving material existence, because as an intermediary it has passed on to the subconscious all of what it has absorbed. In this regard what we term the conscious mind could be compared with a radio which passes on to the listener all of the wonders it broadcasts but is neither what it transmits nor what appreciates it. It is not meant here to discount the dangers of fixation by the subconscious on such stimulus but we will discuss this at length later on.

The conscious portion of the mind works so closely with the material body that it is almost more physical than it is mental. The conscious mind holds in its embrace all other levels of our consciousness and is indeed the outer body of the mind. This level of our mind is also creative, since it links creativity in the material to the mind as a whole. Again, following the patterns set out here, the conscious mind is formed in the image of the subconscious. It is made up of the energy of the realms closest to materiality and forms a close bond between the subconscious mind and the materiality it inhabits. This level of our mind represents the ultimate focus, trapped in time and space. It is the only portion of the mind dependent for its existence upon interaction with materiality.

We look here at the conscious mind, a portion of the whole mind, as it overlaps almost equally the physical and mental realms and wonder why it has no cognizance of the subconscious. By virtue of the conscious mind's intense focus, it becomes self-centered and believes that all that passes from other levels of mind have their origins in itself. That is the chief reason we often have no idea of how our lives are ruled by the subconscious. The conscious mind does not often enough look beyond itself for answers and, like a yardstick, it must be measured by outside sources to judge its accuracy. Using dreams we can see the relationship more clearly.

The dream is that state where the subconscious passes on what the body and its conscious mind have taken it through the previous day. When asleep, the body is relatively inactive, the conscious mind gives over dominance to the subconscious mind, and the conscious mind is very much the observer. Those who work with their dreams have an accurate record of their conscious observations. Much like a computer being taken off-line for backup, the conscious mind is taken off-line nightly, and all that it has experienced is backed up and stored in the subconscious. (Except for continued reference and illustration, we will not delve deeply into the dreaming process.) The Cayce material makes a compelling case that so much can be learned from observing the dream process that the initiate has an enviable conscious knowledge of the subconscious and its relationships. The dream state was referred to by Edgar Cayce as the shadow of life after death. Dreams are rich in symbols, the so-called language of the soul. To build a working relationship with one's dreams is to open a window to eternity and peer out.

As the Word was created in the image of God, so too are our minds in the image of the Word. Each is an expression of that from which it springs into life and is in the image of that portion of mind which gave it life. Here we have a three-dimensional picture of the mind—not three minds but three dimensions of one mind. It has been presented thus to give the reader a better understanding of what it is, as well as what we are. It is important to spend the time to understand this aspect of ourselves for mind is where we will spend eternity.

The human body, for all we know about it, remains the most misunderstood of all material marvels. It is from within our own selves that the soul chooses to work out its destiny in materiality; the body is perfectly suited for this function. What are some of the attributes which suit it so well as a dwelling place for our higher selves? Firstly, our bodies are formed of the elements of the earth and as such find life in its environs very hospitable. The body is suited to interact with all that it encounters in the earth. Next, the Cayce discourses note that the body is so constructed that each of our spiritual attributes has physical counterparts. This enables our soul to more naturally express itself in materiality and, at the same time, not find itself totally confined in the vehicle for its expression. Lastly, the body is flexible. It can evolve and adapt as we grow as souls in the earth.

We have seen that from the beginning there was for us a single creative expression, and from this what was created then expressed itself. Here in materiality, owing to our limited three-dimensional perspective, we have what appears to be a curious route of expression into the physical. It is easy to see creation expressing itself continuously and moving orderly through what it has expressed. The creative process appears less progressive when we see that the physical body was an expression of the Master Soul and then bodies created bodies while other souls manifested through them. There appears to be a break in the smoothness of the stride unless we lift this from the constraints of time and space. Where there is no time, the image moves more orderly and progressively. It is no different than the division of the Word, except that that division is imaged as happening all at once while our time-space perspective creates the illusion that bodies are being created at separate times.

Where in the body does one find the spirit, the will, the mind, the soul? What does it look like and how do we measure it? Science has found that the body is an atomic structure made up of cells forming all of its various members. Bodies are designed to operate in accord with the pattern of their perfection. Each and every cell has a consciousness, it knows its place in the body, and—most important—it knows how to reproduce itself. A cell adheres to the pattern of perfection implanted within it. When there is a condition that upsets its electrical balance, the cell must be resuscitated so that it may regain its conformity with its pattern. So where then does the soul reside in the body? We must here point out that the soul and its forces are not material nor can they be observed by the physical senses. That which is formed of this realm is apparent to the senses of this realm but that which is not can only be observed in materiality by its influence. This is not to minimize psychic perception, which is neither of nor dependent upon the forces of this material realm. Our soul forces occupy the same space as our bodies, although not the same dimension. The Cayce discourses illustrate the order in which they are manifest in the body through the glandular system. This may be surprising because we equate the brain with the mind. But we must take cognizance that the central nervous system, of which the brain is part, is that which carries communication throughout the body. The brain transforms such communication so that the messages are understood by all parts of the body all of the time. Organic in nature, the brain works by electrical impulse resulting in biological activity throughout the body. The reverse is also true, for the brain converts physical senses into impulses which are converted and transmitted along the central nervous system to the glands and from there to the soul.

This is a strange concept, that of the glandular system being the gateway for the soul forces in a living physical body. The Hindu culture has long talked of the chakras, the seven wheel-shaped spiritual centers in the astral body. Not only did the Edgar Cayce discourses agree with the Hindu perspective but went one giant step further and noted that the counterpart of the chakras in a physical body were the seven major glands. Cayce observed that "the glandular forces then are ever akin to the sources from which, through which, the soul dwells within the body." (281-38)

The Cayce discourses give, in great detail, the relationship of the spiritual centers to the ductless glands of the physical body. In order from bottom to top in the physical body, the seven spiritual centers are expressed through the gonads, the lyden, the adrenals, the thymus, the thyroid, the pituitary, and the pineal. In the physical body the first four are associated with physical activities while the higher three are associated with spiritual activities. Through the gonads enters the life force into the body. Through the lyden enters the balance between creativity and spirit amplification (male-female balance). Through the adrenals enter the emotional, the thymus the knowledge of good and evil, and the thyroid the activities of the will. The pineal is the highest physically but second highest spiritually; through this center enters the knowledge of the Word or oneness with all life, while through the pituitary enters the awareness of our oneness with God. Not only are hormones produced by these centers, but the glands resonate to the call of the soul. As the glandular centers resonate they produce a color, not physically but spiritually, visible only to the subconscious forces. Those colors are gonads—red, lyden—orange, solar plexus—yellow, thymus—green, thyroid—blue, pineal—indigo, and pituitary—violet. Students of astrology may recognize these influences as gonads—Saturn, lyden—Neptune, solar plexus—Mars, thymus—Venus, thyroid—Uranus, pineal—Mercury, and pituitary—Jupiter. It is through these glands that the soul and mental forces enter a living human body; and through these same centers all that is gained through the physical senses is recorded in the soul and mental forces. In psychic discourse 281-38, given by Edgar Cayce on the afternoon of October 27, 1937, he said, "For as has been indicated in some manners, some activities, there is an activity within the system produced by anger, fear, mirth, joy, or any of those active forces, that produces through the glandular secretion those activities that flow into the whole of the system." Those activities flowing into the portion of the system we know as the physical body are by this illustration resulting in a physical happening as a direct result of a mental cause. The mental therefore has its effect on the physical through the endocrine system.

Fear, for example, will not make the heart beat faster, but the adrenaline flow which fear produces will definitely affect the heart's rate of pulsation. The glands enable the cells of the body to take from the system that which is needed to reproduce itself, and such reproduction will therefore depend on just what is being impressed upon this system by the mental forces. To the degree that the life force is uninhibited by the mental activity, healthy reproduction will occur. Likewise blockages caused by unproductive attitudes will certainly have their deteriorating effect. Attitudes and emotions are the basis for the relationship between mind and body. It is worth repeating here that the mental forces do not reside in the endocrine system but are akin to and expressed through it.

Now we can begin to see how the mental conditions finally become manifest in the physical body. As the body grows, the first influences which affect it are genetic. As time passes and the mind works with the body, the mental forces have an increasingly greater influence on the body. Gradually the body is conformed to the mental image which is expressed through it, though modified by genetic disposition.

What is a healthy body? What is an unhealthy body? Simply, any body which functions at its optimum is healthy. The body which conforms to the healthy pattern is considered ideal and the body which does not is considered unhealthy. Whether the loss of health is caused by an accident, by mental, genetic, or other conditions, it is essentially the disruption of the atomic forces of the body which causes the physical discord. The restoration which may be brought about through various healing modalities is ultimately that which allows the body to regain its balance and conform to the pattern of perfection existent within each of its cells. Contrary to what we would like to believe, no one can tell the body how to heal itself or knows better than the body how it should function. The body, however, is a structure made up of the elements of the earth and subject to material laws. As a vehicle for the soul it is designed perfectly to express the mental and spiritual forces in the earth. When properly kept, it can do so for quite a long time. When improperly cared for, the body inhibits the soul, which will take its leave of the body sooner rather than later.

Here we have the body, mind, and soul, successive creations, each being an expression of what came before it. Each represents a more intense focus of awareness. Each is an embodiment formed by the same patterns but transforming those patterns to conform to the laws of that dimension in which they are expressed. All of the attributes found in the spirit and mental forces of an individual are also found expressed in the human body. Studies of the works of Rudolf Steiner and Edgar Cayce are particularly useful, because of their detail and clarity, in attaining a better understanding of the successive manifestations of the soul in materiality.

UNIVERSAL LAWS

We have described the body, the mind, and the soul. If we wish to understand their functioning in the earth, we must understand the laws which shape materiality. Life in the earth was designed to be an orderly growing experience. The physical realm was imaged as a dimension with very special qualities, in a universe of dimensions. The entire realm and all it contains are held in place by forces we call universal laws. Our lives here and, in fact, time and space would not exist without them. Fortunately universal laws are unchangeable even though we often wish they were not. Humankind's laws, which are designed to maintain order, are not perfect and poorly mimic God's laws. In a sense these laws are counterfeit, since they do not apply to all of us equally and they often carry benefits or penalties only when others witness our compliance with or indifference toward them. Universal laws work the same for all people all of the time and require no witness. They are in fact the very patterns of universal life through which spirit is expressed in materiality. Universal laws issue forth from the angelic realms, having been drawn from patterns in higher realities. They are then being transformed, expressed in all of the dimensions that are tied to and surround materiality.

Bruce McArthur did an exhaustive study of universal laws as described in the Edgar Cayce psychic discourses. McArthur developed a course on the subject which will long be a model for students of such laws. Nowhere else is there currently so large a study, so deep in understanding, and so articulately conveyed as in his universal laws course. Much of what is presented here on universal laws is based on McArthur's work, which is summarized in his book, *Your Life: Why It Is the Way It Is and What You Can Do About It.*

There are hundreds of universal laws but we will here go over what we consider to be the major divisions under which the rest might fall. Those divisions are Like Begets Like, As You Sow So Shall You Reap, Law of Us, Law of Expectancy, Law of Attraction, Law of Chance, Law of Cause and Effect, Law of Abundance, Law of Karma, Law of Grace, Law of Mercy, Law of Love, Law of Truth, and the Law of One. One could make a case that all laws are part of the Law of Love but that would not help us to better understand them. The Edgar Cayce discourses repeatedly noted that God is Love. As all things are manifestations of God, all things are likewise manifestations of love. Rather than overwhelming ourselves with something so large that we could not productively relate to it, let us look at these universal laws individually.

Like Begets Like
That like flows from like things is a basic principle of life. We could not grow apples from papaya seeds nor can good flow from bad. This ever so simple universal law is one we deny a thousand times a day. No thing, no thought, no deed, no activity can give rise to something that it itself is not. How often have we heard someone excuse an activity because it was designed to bring about some virtue that the act essentially was not. Lies will not bring about truth, violence will not bring about compassion, dishonesty will not bring about ethical behavior, and indifference will not bring about love. We often go through life so intent on bringing things about that we forget to do the very things we wish to result. If we would have joy we must be joyous, for love we must be loving, for peace and harmony we must make peace with ourselves and others, for cooperation we must be cooperative. Any other method of creation is manipulative and inevitably will fail. For the results of manipulation are

deceit, and from this no permanent good can flow. When we can embrace Like Begets Like as a basic underlying principle, life will not become instantly easier. But we will then have a productive direction in which to grow. As we conform our activities to this law, patience will take on a new meaning for each of us, and we will begin living according to this pattern by which our God created the universe.

As You Sow So Shall You Reap

When this law reaches across lifetimes it is called karma. A first cousin to Like Begets Like, this law has much to do with the result of our activities in the earth. We are in the earth now largely to experience the result of our own activities, and this is the law which makes that possible. This principle permeates all levels of reality and although it is anchored in materiality, it is manifest throughout reality. It has special prominence in the earth because of its relationship to our journey here. This law is one with which we cause ourselves a great deal of difficulty. If cause and effect, which we will discuss later, is to have any means of expression it must be in As You Sow So Shall You Reap.

Often we lack the patience to work with this law because we expect instantly to reap what we have sown. Spiritual activity needs time to unfold in the mental and material activities. As previously noted, little comes into life fully grown, and growth is certainly evident throughout creation. Time and space allow for us to perceive this growth in measured amounts; therefore, we cannot expect instant results when we work with this law. We can expect to experience ourselves, and know that if we feel the victim of life, we are the perpetrator as well. Likewise, our good fortune is likely the result of forces we have also set in motion. In creation, where laws work perfectly, there are no accidents or the laws which hold life together would be imperfect themselves. We can and do build our own futures by As You Sow So Shall You Reap.

The Law of Us

We are all interconnected and no one can experience anything without its affecting us all. All life is interrelated and all souls are linked by heritage, awareness, mission, and destiny. Earlier we discussed the collective consciousness of all souls and that state of oneness to which we strive to return. In the earth we have the unique opportunity to work in community for the benefit of others. When we speak unkindly of others, when we judge our fellow souls, when we strive at the expense of others, we run in opposition of this Law of Us. In a psychic discourse on the subject, Edgar Cayce said, "There is so much good in the worst of us, and so much bad in the best of us, it doesn't behoove any of us to speak evil of the rest of us. This is a universal law, and until one begins to make application of same, one may not go very far in spiritual or soul development." (3063-1)

When we bring into the lives of others fruits of the spirit—which are peace, harmony, brotherly love, patience, kindness, gentleness, hope, and faith—all living souls, because of our connectedness, are nourished by our activities and we become the law we are expressing. It is not sufficient only to have knowledge of the law, but it must be expressed in our daily doings. The Law of Us, which springs from the oneness of all souls, is best expressed in the earth by helping others.

The Law of Expectancy

Mind is ever the builder and few things are as potent for the mind as expectancy. When we work with cause and effect, which will be discussed later in this chapter, expectancy builds in both the mental realms and the material ones. This law works so well that often we give material expression to our worst fears. What we expect must be consistent with our activities, or the discord blocks its manifestation. This is not wishing and having it fulfilled; this is living in a manner consistent with expectancy. The Law of Expectancy is the application of faith, without which little good can ever result. Many among us think that faith can do all things. But faith must be lived, until it is so made part of a life that it is expectancy. What turns faith into expectancy is living according to that faith. What makes expectancy a reality is universal law.

The Law of Attraction

Outside of the earth Like Begets Like deals with the process of creation, while the Law of Attraction deals with that already created. In the earth Like Begets Like deals mostly with attitudes and emotions, while the Law of Attraction deals largely with people and things. The relationship of how these laws manifest in, as well as outside of, materiality helps us to understand how individual patterns take on different forms.

All of life vibrates at particular frequencies. Those which vibrate at similar frequencies attract each other and together they form harmonies. Opposites work against the vibrational patterns of each other and the result is often discord and chaos. This law works whether we are consciously aware of it or not. Like people attract, like creation attracts, and like mindedness attracts. We, each of us, carry an encapsulated history of ourselves in an energy field which surrounds us, as that which we call an aura. We respond to it even though we do not physically see it with any of our five senses. Those things which we recognize and find attractive draw us to others just as those things we find in opposition to ourselves repel us. Working with conscious and subconscious memories, we are attracted to places and things. Once vibrations are in accord, life seeks out its own.

The Law of Chance

This is a rather peculiar but interesting law. Essentially, nothing happens by chance. We may, in materiality, call chance good or bad luck, good or bad fortune, destiny, or by any other terminology we care to use. No matter what we term it, chance does not operate by divine law—it does not operate at all. Chance is an illusion and as such it is an escape from responsibility.

It is difficult to accept how absolutely the Law of Chance denies the existence of a value embraced in one form or another by most of the world. This law would tell us that coincidences are not by chance but by design. They are the result of activities set in motion previously to bring about desired results. When the entire universe comes to our aid and we observe it as repetitive events, it is often called synchronicity. Synchronicity calls our attention to a structured situation rather than events as random happenings. We hope for good luck, an unearned and largely undeserved reward. We avoid misfortune, an equally unearned consequence. In this attempted escape from reality the universe will not help us. We proceed largely by illusion, or we must take responsibility for the events, all of the events in our lives. We must begin to deal with all we encounter as being the result of our own activities, and then we are working with the Law of Chance. Outside of materiality this law manifests as forces which keep order in the affairs of God's creatures.

The Law of Cause and Effect

Although no universal law takes prominence over another, this one is of particular importance to us in the earth. Cause and effect strikes closer to our hearts from an earthly perspective because it is the foundation upon which our material dimension rests. Simply defined, all that is has its cause; the converse of this is that all activity has its effect. There is nothing we can do that will not manifest in reality, and again there is nothing we experience that we have not had a hand in causing. Like all other laws, this one is immutable; it works the same for all and does so all of the time. We have often come to think of the law of materiality as the law of fairness. We prefer to see this dimension being held together by our widely varied perspectives of what is fair and unfair. Fairness is a material perspective; it differs from individual to individual, it has nothing to do with universal law, and it could best be described as an inconsistent, man-made value. From time to time we believe the earth is founded upon other laws such as love, peace, mercy, knowledge, joy, and so on. All of these (although not all are laws) are present in materiality and work exceedingly well—some work even better outside of our physical reality. Nowhere else in creation is cause and effect in the position of dominance as it is in the earth. This is hard to accept because it exacts certain behavioral patterns from each of us. It makes us responsible for all of the things that hurt us and that cry out for change in our lives. The promise here is that we can make a difference as we change reality.

The first six laws outlined here operate in materiality because and only because of the Law of Cause and Effect. So dominant is cause and effect that it is a law itself as well as a catalyst for other laws. When we take responsibility for the things around us, when hope springs into life from our hearts, when we begin to act upon these, we have begun to mature in our relationship with universal laws and particularly the Law of Cause and Effect. Outside of materiality this law works in concert with the will forces in creation. It is creative and works most closely with the principles of growth.

The Law of Abundance

This is the fun law, for we all want abundance. It is elu-
sive to many, and one which requires careful study.
There is much about this law which appears inconsistent, but if anything is out of order, it is our perception.
This law is an extension of the Law of Love. To understand this law we must first understand that we own
nothing. All that we have or ever will have is entrusted
into our care. Supply, all supply of any kind, belongs to
our God and therefore it is infinite. There is no shortage,
no end, and consequently there is no lack in the universe. Further, all abundance is made by the Creator exclusively for the created.

Abundance flows more freely where there is room to
receive it. When we give what has been placed in our
care, we draw additional supply. If we try to draw on
abundance directly, we are in opposition to this law, but
when we begin the free flow by giving, we conform to
the law. Let us look at it this way: If we push toward others, this generates the healthy pull upon supply; but if
we pull directly toward ourselves, we are severely limited in what we can draw. The Law of Abundance can just
as accurately be called the law of giving because of the
direction (pushing) the use of this law must take.

We must understand that this law works with all supply, and when working with it, one must be consistent.
There is spiritual supply, mental supply, and physical
supply. We cannot successfully work with abundance on
one level and ignore it on others. Without consistency
our efforts to work with this law will have little success.
Motive, attitude, and action must all be in accord with
unselfishness if we are to have the proper tools to build
with this law. One particular lesson from the prophet
Malachi is a moving discourse on the Law of Abundance
which promises, "Bring ye all the tithes into the storehouse, that there may be meat in mine house, and prove

me now herewith . . . if I will not open you the windows
of heaven, and pour you out a blessing, that there shall
not be room enough to receive it." (Mal. 3:10) There are
many passages in the Bible which encourage giving and
extol its virtues, but nowhere else in that work will we
find the challenge so bold and direct. The Law of Abundance works outside of the earth, where there generally
is no concern of shortage, more in the appearance of the
Law of Giving. Outside of materiality, the more we give,
the greater grows the capacity to give.

The Law of Karma

Here we have a law that is widely misunderstood, especially by students of New Age philosophy. For the most
part, karma is thought of as punishment. But it is no
such thing. It is a blessing rather than a curse. As hard as
it is to believe, karma is a first cousin to the Law of Grace.
Simply stated, karma is the experiencing of self from one
life to the next. There is personal karma, group karma,
and even national karma. Individuals and groups of individuals experience karma much the same. We incarnate into groups such as families, communities, cities,
states, regions, nations, races, and the like. We often have
the opportunity to experience ourselves not only as individuals but as groups as well. We can have pleasant
experiences or unpleasant ones depending upon what
we have built in our earthly lives to experience. We have
here what can be considered a law combining As You
Sow So Shall You Reap with cause and effect across lifetimes in the earth. We build experiences in our lives, and
where it is beneficial to relive the results of our experiences, we do so through the Law of Karma.

Throughout our experiences we have built helpful as
well as hurtful conditions. We draw upon the strengths
built from the helpful ones to deal with the difficulties
resulting from the hurtful ones. It is by the mercy of an

all-loving God that we will deal with and overcome all of the difficulties we have built into our memories. We can accept the full force of grace to overcome and find healing, or we can accept a limited portion of grace and be healed by the experience itself. Either way we are healed of the experience and we can move on. Often we choose to hide from the damage we do, so that living the results not only captures our attention but enables us to deal with and overcome our misdeeds. How do we do this? By what we do with what we meet. It is that simple. Part and parcel to the memory of the difficulty caused, we bring with us to each situation exactly that which we need to constructively deal with it. There is no deed, no experience, no karma we meet that we do not have the ability to deal with. This is part of the blessings of a time-measured dimension, that we need not face all of ourselves at any single time. Here we may gradually deal with ourselves only in that amount we can constructively handle at the time. We will see in subsequent chapters how in other realms the experiences we built in materiality continue to help us grow.

The Law of Grace

Probably the most well known of all universal laws is this one. This law walks hand in hand with the Law of Mercy. Here we have unconditional and unearned forgiveness from an infinitely loving and merciful Father. A unique quality of this law is that it places no condition upon us and as such it cannot be earned. We do however need to accept grace, or it is of no help to us. Grace is given once and for all and is accessible to each one all of the time. Most of us do not accept all of grace at any single time, but this does not lessen or in any way diminish the perfection of this law. You may ask why would anyone not accept any portion of grace, which is priceless and costs us nothing. We refuse grace because we do not yet wish to give up those things we hold so close that need forgiveness. Think of it; before you have had a chance to exact any price for the wrongs you have suffered, you must give up the anger. Just short of fame and fortune, you must give up your moment of personal glory. We have become so accustomed to fear and doubt that we find great security in their continued influence in our lives.

The Law of Grace reaches out to us throughout all eternity in every level of reality. It pulls ever at us and never for a single moment in eternity relaxes its draw upon us. Grace enters every condition, every situation, and every activity in which we can find ourselves. There is nothing we have ever or will ever experience in which grace does not reside in full measure.

The Law of Mercy

Mercy implies compassion. Albert Nolan *Jesus Before Christianity* notes that the man Jesus had a single focal point from which His ministry flowed; it was His boundless compassion for others. Without this compassion, Nolan implies, it is not likely Jesus would have been impelled to become one with the Christ.

Mercy is accessible to us all; it is manifest on all levels and it is only a thought away from each of us. We likewise have the opportunity to draw upon this attribute and express it everywhere in our lives. All of us have at one time or another received mercy, and it is not likely that even the worst of us have not shown mercy. No reasonably balanced person wants not to be shown mercy, but many of us become so confused we forget to show it ourselves. Each time we show mercy we build this attribute into ourselves as it passes through us. If we show mercy often enough, we build an abundance of it into our own fabric and become as one with it. Outside of the earth the Law of Mercy impels each of us to feel tender lovingkindness toward all of creation.

The Law of Love

We are at the root of universal law when we look at love. There is an interesting quote from the Edgar Cayce psychic discourses which states that "law is love, love is law, God is Love." (900-20) This seems to imply that God, love, and law are one and the same. At closer inspection we see that the psychic held that the nearest single thing in spirituality which is closest to the nature of God is love. Further, law is a manifestation of God, drawn from love, and it is transformed into universal laws.

There is yet another insightful quotation from the Cayce work which sheds much light on the Law of Love. "Those who give ungrudgingly, those who give willingly of themselves that others may attain, that others may have the opportunity to learn and know good, that purity, that love, that unselfishness exists in a material world, are complying with the law of love . . . Thus such individuals through the law of love receive joy and happiness in return." (5018-1) The Law of Love is that by which, through which, the nature of God is materially and spiritually manifest. All unselfishness, all kindness are expressions of the Law of Love. This law binds all of spirituality one to another and is the foundation for all goodness.

The Law of Truth

Truth is infinitely more than honesty. On a spiritual level knowledge is knowing ourselves to be ourselves and yet one with God, while truth is experiencing knowledge. Truth to each of us on a personal level is a changing condition. As we grow in awareness, so does truth. As we apply universal laws both spiritually and materially, truth is the result. Truth is the living spirit, the life which emanates from the will acting upon life in a lawful fashion. In spiritual realms the Spirit of Truth is seen as the light which illuminates reality. In materiality it is a life lived lawfully. We bring light into any situation where we manifest truth. By living by and with the universal laws, by living a life which is moved by the Spirit of God, by living in accord with all we were meant to be, we become the Truth and the Light.

The Law of One

The great Jewish prayer known simply as the Shema, after the first word in it, is Shema Yisrael, Adonoi Elohenu, Adonoi Echaud (Hear, O Israel, the Lord our God, the Lord is One). All life is one life and it is all a manifestation of the one God. Not only is all life made of the same substance, but it is all connected. There is no realm where this law does not dominate, and in fact even the various realms of reality are connected by it one with the other. In the earth we must grow in the knowledge that what we do affects all living things. We cannot hurt someone without hurting everyone. We cannot treat any part of the earth poorly and not have it affect all of nature adversely. When an animal or a plant becomes extinct, we lose a vital balance to life in the earth forever. In reality, no form of life, in whatever realm it resides, exists apart from all life in all realms. When we experience this, we experience the Law of One.

The Whole Law

Combining excerpts from Matthew 22:37 and the Edgar Cayce discourses concerning this law we have " 'Thou shalt love the Lord thy God with all thy heart, thy mind, thy body; thy neighbor as thyself.' This as He gave is the whole law. There is none above that." (348-1) The Whole Law is the synthesis of all other laws. The Whole Law is the whole purpose in any experience and on a universal level it is the whole experience in creation. This law exists largely the same in all dimensions—to bring together all of the law as it is expressed in that reality.

We could write an entire book on the fourteen universal laws discussed here and volumes of books on those which have not been. An exhaustive study of universal laws is not our purpose. They have been presented in their abbreviated form to give the reader a basic understanding of those laws which hold reality together and of how they are expressed in creation. Of course, it is important to our journey to understand how they guide life in the earth. But they are presented here so that we can see how such patterns of life are expressed throughout creation.

GROWTH

Neither we nor any other of God's creations come into being full grown. In nature we have countless examples of this principle, as we have also in our own personal lives. This is a pattern which is manifest throughout all of creation, that the created will grow to fulfill its position in the body of the whole. We are born as children who grow in physical attributes, and of particular importance, we grow in awareness. Observation teaches us that nature, the animal kingdom, the vegetable, and even the mineral are also evolving; the planet itself is evolving.

Let us briefly touch upon mineral growth because it escapes the awareness of much of humankind. We look at the elements of the earth and think that they have always been. But geology tells us something different. This planet, we are told, was in a molten state and cooled into the various material elements to which we have become accustomed. All elements were present in the molten state but had not yet crystallized. When eventually a cooling of the surface took place, the minerals crystallized into matter of simple and compound elements. If nothing else, this indicates millions of years of growth of the minerals. We do not look upon minerals as having an awareness, so we stop right here and say that the elements are now formed. This view is myopic because we deny the elements of the earth that sense of self that we allow to all other life on the planet. How could a rock which has been a rock for one hundred million years have a sense of self, how could it be growing? Unlike in animal life, the answer is outside of the elements instead of within them. The awareness of the mineral kingdom is manifest in other dimensions and not in the object itself. There is more than just a mineral awareness but a growing living intelligence of its place in creation and its destiny as one with the whole. Unlike us, a mineral does not have the ability to choose for itself. So it has never been out of touch with its Creator and all of creation. In her *Angels Sing,* Dorothy Maclean writes that there are manifest creatures of awareness, beings, angels, or what she calls devas. They draw upon life itself from the higher realms of creation and transform them in the earth as part of the mineral kingdom. In addition they hold mineral life together so it does not just dissipate and evaporate. Matter is not just something which was created once and then takes on its own being; it is something which has evolved and must be kept in existence. The elements of the earth are manifestations of their Creator and therefore they live. They are living spirit transformed into simple and complex forms of matter. The mineral consciousness lies within the devic kingdom, from which flows their newly transformed life. As intelligent, living forms of life, minerals grow in many of the ways we do, with the two exceptions we have pointed out. First, their consciousness resides outside of their material form; and second, they must remain true to their purpose as they cannot choose to do otherwise. They therefore do not experience karma because such a law is part of the ability to choose.

Plant life or the vegetable kingdom lies between the mineral and animal kingdoms. There is more awareness of self within the material structure than there is within the mineral, but not as full an occupancy as in the animal kingdom. Again, there are those realms where higher forms of vegetable consciousness exist as a collective, creative awareness. Because the physical growth of the members of the vegetable kingdom are incalculably quicker than of the mineral, its growth is more easily observed in a time and space perspective. Here we see the growth from seed to full bloom and back again to the elements of the earth. Growth in awareness is no different from the mineral kingdom and likewise the vegetable awareness is not corrupted through erroneous choices. Again, only the human species has the ability to choose and therefore the vegetable is always on the right path in its evolutionary journey. The vegetable knows its position in creation as well as its ultimate destiny.

One may ask why vegetable life dies short of its full fruitage or is distorted and deformed from its perfect pattern. Why, if it has not corrupted itself, does it become less than it was created to be? The answer lies in what human souls have done to the natural forces rather than what these forces have done to themselves.

Growth is not limited only to those forms of life which can choose, for all life grows and only we have the ability to choose. Growth is the assimilation, the accumulation of experience, and this is the heritage of all of creation in whatever reality it may be found. Guiding this principle is the Law of Truth.

Next we have the most complex form of creation, the animal kingdom. We find the consciousness of its non-human members manifest in its material form and its growth can easily be observed physically and mentally. There are those realms, discussed by Dorothy Maclean, where messengers of God guide animal creation. They care for the regenerative patterns of these animal creatures as well as guard the laws that govern their lives. These messengers are protectors, so to speak, of the collective consciousness of the various animal species, and the very awareness of these angelic beings forms a dimension from which animal life emanates. Like other life forms, the nonhuman animal kingdom does not have freedom of choice at its core and therefore is in touch with its place in creation. Even though the animal does not experience karma, it does, like its human counterpart, reincarnate in materiality in the earth. Edgar Cayce pointed out that here in the earth there is no transmigration where a human can reincarnate as an animal or an animal as a human. He further noted that there is, however, animal incarnation where its life force can be expressed in a variety of animal forms from one incarnation to another. This is part of the pattern of nonhuman animal growth. Because animals do store experiences in their subconscious, they retain memories as they grow, largely through accumulated experiences.

We have a tendency to become attached to animals. The potency of our mental forces, Cayce noted, draws to us those animals with whom we may have had experiences in the past. This is not their karmic choice; it is ours magnetically impressed upon them. As in the vegetable kingdom, any imperfection we see in these creatures has its basis in humankind. The nonhuman animal kingdom consists of members closest to ourselves.

Souls in human form are the focal point of their own entire consciousness. It is from within the physical body that all of our consciousness is accessible. We note the stages of consciousness embodiment, first the mineral whose entire awareness is from without, then to the vegetable which has almost equal parts of its awareness residing within as well as without itself, then the nonhuman animal kingdom whose consciousness resides mostly within its physical form, and then souls incarnate in human form whose entire consciousness resides within their form. It is here where the drama of soul growth in the earth takes place, within the soul's physical being. The body is the soul's exquisitely designed medium for conscious growth.

We move into this dimension born in a body which must grow in capacity to function, as well as with a newly acquired conscious mind which must grow in awareness of the laws of the earth. This pattern of creation, when expressed in the earth, decrees that growth must be gradual. It would be well to question the necessity for slow growth, when we are in each earth incarnation for such a relatively short period of time. Growth arises out of the process of human experience and not from the completion of it. Whether we soar to the heights or sink to the depths is not of itself relevant. Growth comes in the actual movement and as such it is best accomplished, when in a time and space realm, by gradual movement. It is part of why we have chosen to work in this dimension, that we can take full advantage of meeting all things gradually. We do this so that we may have the fullest benefit of the process of all we experience.

Next, one might logically ask why repeat the formative years from birth to sixteen or seventeen when most of the important process will take place thereafter. Simply, we have not yet used to their optimum the stages of infancy, adolescence, and adulthood. If we used each well, conforming to the pattern of life in the earth, we would find no need to return. Further, to be born fully aware would be a total reversal of the pattern of growth as it manifests in the earth.

It is important to acknowledge here that what we perceive to be a gradual growth in awareness, as well as capacity, follows us in all realms. An understanding of this single concept will help us to better understand how we as souls develop in other realms of awareness. This is clearly one of those telltale patterns which help us to understand the continuity of the Spirit of Life as it manifests throughout reality. As we set out in the beginning to emphasize the continuity of patterns even though they be expressed differently, we must now give equal emphasis to growth being gradual. The mission on which we find ourselves is one which we perceive to be an upward movement to oneness with our creator and creation. This oneness comes about not in an instant but as the result of growth from experiences. Through the Spirit of Truth we may become lights in the body of God.

BIRTH, DEATH, AND DYING

"I am standing upon the seashore. A ship at my side spreads her white sails to the morning breeze and starts for the blue ocean.

"She is an object of beauty and strength, and I stand and watch her until at length she is only a speck of white cloud just where the sea and sky meet and mingle with each other. Then someone at my side exclaims, 'There, she is gone!'

"Gone where? Gone from my sight, that is all. She is just as large in hull and mast and spar as she was when she left my side, and just as able to bear her load of living freight to the place of her destination. Her diminished size is in me, not in her.

"And just at that moment when someone at my side says, 'She is gone,' there are other eyes watching for her coming and other voices ready to take up the glad shout, 'There, she comes!'

"And that is dying."   (Author unknown)

In a very real sense being born into the earth is like dying. We leave awareness and residence in one reality and forsake them to enter another. We reside in realms outside of materiality and enjoy a wider perception than experienced in the earth. We will not discuss these realms at length here as they will be described in greater detail in later chapters. Our focus outside of the material realms, as described by Emanuel Swedenborg, is wider and inward, but upon entering material reality the focus becomes narrower and outward. At first what we have just noted seems contradictory. One would imagine spiritual realms as relatively outward and material realms as relatively inward. Our erroneous perception is the result of our acceptance of greater reality as being outside, beyond the universe.

Let us illustrate here for a better understanding. One should imagine a glass filled with water in the middle of the ocean. The glass is inverted, held upside down and mostly above the water. The water will not run out so long as the open part, which was the top and is now at the bottom, is held under the water. Now we place a box over the glass of water, completely surrounding its entire portion above the top of ocean's surface. Imagine that the box is one hundred miles tall, one hundred miles wide, and one hundred miles deep. Inside of this box exactly at the center is the inverted glass of water and inside of the glass, above the ocean's surface is a drop of water that has recently become aware of itself. As the drop of water looks up and out, the expanse before it seems infinite. The self-aware drop can see that there is a universe of sorts above the glass but can't distinguish the details because the water around it obscures its vision and the outside expanse is so large. The water drop then concludes that to penetrate the borders which contain it and to rise upward is to move into the great expanse of eternity. It does not occur to the water that if it turned within the glass and receded into the ocean, the ocean itself would offer a greater reality than exists inside of the box; and once in the ocean, if it could move beyond the box and be transformed into vapor, it would become a part of a realm unimaginably larger than that which existed inside the box and larger than had existed within the ocean. For this drop of water, further into itself would take it into the greater reality and outside of itself would take it to a lesser reality. One would not expect the water to prefer moving from the vast expanse above the earth, into the ocean, through the box, and inside of the glass; but if our illustration is to parallel birth, this is exactly what must occur.

Here we have the soul in mental realms moving into material realms in order to gain the focus necessary to complete its mission. At this point it is not necessary that the soul lose all of its awareness of the estate it held before material incarnation, and this loss is gradual. Let us try to imagine the first moments of physical life and the transformation of consciousness which occurs. We enter materiality and the physical senses are overwhelming. The sensation of material manifestation is like a combination of pain all over, inside and out, coupled with a paralyzing heaviness. The brightness of physical light cuts through our senses like a white knife and the discordant sounds add an entirely new dimension to the pain we are suffering. The vibrations around us have lost all rhythm, and we must fight to keep our own life force from resonating to this chaotic pulsation. We are completely disoriented and suffering incredible trauma. The odors are bizarre and the tastes are sickening. The breath of life no longer flows freely through us; we must have air and our newly formed body is heaving for its next breath. How paradoxical it seems that for this horror we left eternity and higher realms of consciousness.

It takes all of our conscious focus to bear this assault;

it is exhausting. Little by little we move deeper and deeper into materiality as our agony exacts more and more of our concentration. Little by little we move further away from the broader focus we had before physical birth. Our only relief from this assault of physical sensation comes in sleep, and we take advantage of that brief respite at every opportunity. Now begins the task of learning, assimilation, and application. More and more we invest our awareness in the state we occupy and the tasks at hand. The lessons we have learned before will have to be learned again and somehow it does not seem any easier, even though we have done this many times before. It will take years to control this awkward, difficult-to-use structure we call a body and to become accustomed to this smothering confinement.

How ironic it is that from this ominous beginning we become so firmly anchored in this materiality that we fight beyond reason to retain our contact with it. Gradually, as we learn, as we grow, we lose sight of our immortality and believe that our being like everything else is tied to material existence. The father of modern philosophy, René Descartes, poetically summed up his being by noting, "I think, therefore I am." Gradually we move from this greater reality to one which embodies the lesser awareness of "I physically sense and this is what I am." So attached will we become to these senses, so much will we identify with them, that gradually we will lose sight of where our being stops and our sensing begins. As a result of our confusion we will grow in the fear that to surrender our physical senses is to surrender our being.

From the very beginning we start to modify this structure we occupy. We impress our image upon the body, and throughout our lives the body conforms to it. The developing conscious mind adjusts amazingly quickly and takes its rightful, dominant position unchallenged. The sentient mind is suitably at home in the growing body and is very much a part of it. Strangely enough, the subconscious and superconscious minds never do find comfort in the body, and, as Edgar Cayce noted, throughout physical incarnation they take their leave of it frequently. In that state we call sleep, where the conscious mind gives over its dominant position to the subconscious mind, often our immortal self flees to eternal realms. Those who have developed a working relationship with their subconscious dream selves have had a glimpse of eternity at such times of escape.

The growing self has so much influence over its own development that if we came to know how much, we would find it hard to accept. The mind can deform, heal, or otherwise modify the body to conform to exactly those conditions it chose to work with. The mind can even change the gender of the body in early years or can decide to permanently take its leave and depart without consequence. Edgar Cayce in discourse 1648-2 noted that a five-day-old child felt it had fulfilled its mission and its soul took its leave of materiality. In another discourse, 480-37, Cayce noted that another soul simply changed its mind and turned back at birth.

This is an excellent time to discuss the little understood and painful circumstance of infant death. There are numerous causes of death in young children but they may be divided into three distinct reasons or categories.

The first reason for children's death, which we have just noted, is a change of mind. In most instances the incarnating soul chooses where and when it will incarnate. Family, social conditions, heredity are all influencing factors in the soul's choice. Karma is the key factor in the soul's choice. One might think that if family and social conditions are choices of incarnating souls, we would all be born to intelligent, healthy, good-looking, wealthy parents of high social standing. Some choices may challenge certain faculties, but not all choices are universally helpful. We generally reincarnate in groups so that we can work out unresolved relationships. At the same time we draw strength from certain relationships. We have come to call group reincarnation group karma. Also, certain lifestyles offer distinct challenges at certain times and particular physical conditions are more appropriate for us to complete our chosen task. In some cases an incarnating soul finds that for some reason it chose inappropriately; at that time it is free to change its mind and leave. As the result of such a departure the child will simply expire. Several such cases are found in the Cayce discourses.

The second basic category for children's death is karmic. Hard as it is to accept, there are distinct lessons to be learned from being snatched from our opportunities before we have had occasion to use them. What may appear as a premature death can be an excellent arena for karma and conformity to this universal law. Let us use an example of someone who in a previous incarnation denied others the freedom to use their opportunities. Perhaps the soul was someone who was so overbearing that they stole the potential of others. Is it not merciful that they themselves have the opportunity to experience the result of their own shortcomings? If life is eternal, what is an incarnation cut short before it appears to even begin, when the benefit will last forever? A related reason for children's death (still karmic) is as a service to the group in which the soul chooses to incarnate. There are many ways the death of a child can be helpful to the loving family who survives the child. The incarnating soul may choose to help others by incarnating for only a short period of time. We have all seen families pull together and their character grow in gigantic proportions as the result of illness or death of a child. Again, an incarnation barely lived is not a loss if such a sacrifice leaves behind an eternal blessing. There are several such cases found in the Cayce discourses.

The third and last basic reason for children's death is one of routing. More simply described, it would be the route the soul travels to get from one realm to another. It is myopic to assume that we grow through progressive planes of consciousness from bottom to top or vice versa. Spirituality does not work in progressive layers of geometric form; this is purely an earthly perspective and has no place in greater reality. Growth in spirit is not in a straight line. To become fixed on this idea is to form spirit in the image of matter. Realms overlap, they are in motion and not always in the same proximity to one another. We have excellent examples of this by looking at the earth and our own solar system. If we deal with the planets as if they are realms, we can see that they are not always in the same relative position from one another. If we arrange the planets in a straight line stretching out from the Sun, we see them in a specific position that they rarely occupy. If we measure the distance between the planets Earth and Jupiter while they are in this seldom achieved straight line, we would find them approximately 600,000,000 kilometers apart. Earth moves a much shorter distance to revolve around the Sun and does not rotate at the same speed as Jupiter. Nor does Jupiter's speed of rotation make up for the longer distance it must travel around the Sun. Therefore we do not see all of the planets in a straight line whipping around the Sun, always keeping the same distance from one another. There are even times when Earth and Jupiter are on opposite sides of the Sun, significantly increasing their distance from each other. This is an extreme example of how dimensions in motion often do not occupy the same proximity one to the other. There are times when if we wished to go from Earth to Jupiter, the trip would be much shorter to orbit a planet which would be moving much closer to Jupiter before it again regained its relatively shorter distance from Earth. Mercury, for example, will align with Jupiter far sooner than will Earth. This comparison is particularly important because our movement through spiritual realms is not always in a direct line through overlapping dimensions.

Now, we should bear in mind that distance is not a factor in spirit but proximity is. As we have no time and space in spiritual realms, it is the relationship which one dimension has to another which is the overriding factor in determining proximity. There are occasions where we cannot move in spirit in what we in materiality would call a straight line, and we must move through reality in a more circuitous fashion. Such a direction can easily take place when a soul moving from one reality to another does so by utilizing materiality as a springboard. The soul's purpose in such an incarnation would not be to experience a life in the earth but to use this dimension's proximity to other realms to travel more efficiently. Emanuel Swedenborg, in *Heaven and Its Wonders and Hell from Things Heard and Seen,* notes, "Adults passing on go to places that correspond to their material lives, children do not."

We cannot here quantify by total or percentage which is the greatest reason for death in very young children. The categories are given to impart a better understanding of why lives appear to be cut short prematurely when children die. We will not dwell further upon the death of young children; instead, we will return to the experiences of those who have remained in the earth beyond their fourth year.

We learn in the earth through experience and thus grow. As we act upon life, we build the experience into our bodies, minds, and souls. Likewise we are building our affections to those conditions beyond earthly life. This will determine in part where we will find ourselves after experiencing that change in awareness called death. This "where" will be discussed at great length in later chapters. Our lives are governed by material laws while we dwell in the earth; what we do with them will follow us for a long time after this experience. We will become attached to materiality and all that we have so focused upon. If such affinity is not released in matter, it must be done so in spirit. It will, however, prove to be a much more difficult task to release material fixation in spirit, rather than do so when we can freely use to its optimum the law of cause and effect.

Life in the earth is not only experiencing ourselves, within the confines of universal laws, but it is done in a much more focused fashion. As we live in the earth plane we are at the same time building conditions in succeeding realms. The building process in materiality is therefore multidimensional. The Edgar Cayce source expressed it best in discourse 5749-3 when the entranced psychic stated, " . . . with error entered that as called *death*, which is only a transition—or through God's other door—into that realm where the entity has builded, in its manifestations as related to the knowledge and activity respecting the law of the universal influence."

As all of life is a gradual metamorphosis, so is that period of transition we call dying. From a physical perspective we might say one was alive one moment and gone the next. We may comment that death came without warning. Because we see only those external happenings which are perceptible to the physical senses, we often assume there was no activity outside of this perspective. As we grow in stages from infancy to maturity, we likewise grow from life in material realms to life in spiritual dimensions. The pattern here is ever the same: We do not instantly arrive at, occupy, or depart from any condition in reality. Dying is a process which begins before the soul takes leave of the body and in fact begins before any illness, accident, or happening which may cause physical death. In that rest we call sleep, the soul departs and prepares for the transition it is moving toward. How far in advance of our departure do we begin our preparations? In a sense, one is preparing for death throughout all of life. Again, let us refer to the Cayce work and psychic discourse 5488-1 which states, " . . . in the midst of life one is in the midst of death, for death is but the beginning of life, as life is but the *beginning* of an opportunity to manifest that as is *innately* built within the soul of an individual itself." Even though our earthly lives are in part a preparation for death, as we move closer to that transition we prepare more intensely. Remember the law of chance: Nothing happens by chance. For every effect there is a cause, and for those things which affect our own lives, we are the cause. It is not possible to hide our death from ourselves; therefore, we seize the opportunity to prepare with more fervor as we move closer.

The way we die is particularly important, not the cause so much as the process. Steiner and Cayce agree that we begin preparation for our imminent transition at a particular point where we have either completed what we came into the earth in this particular experience to accomplish, or when there is no longer any possibility of any further growth in this physical lifetime. This inability to grow further in a lifetime could be due to physical, mental, or emotional conditions or a combination of factors. None of us will find ourselves in the earth a moment longer than necessary to use the experience productively. When we have reached that condition where to remain incarnate in materiality holds no further promise of growth, the God of mercy has willed that we are to be set free. This may be difficult to accept, as we apparently do not lack for living examples of those who are so misguided that they seem beyond hope. Perhaps we are also misguided in our opinions of our fellows; for while their deeds may be repulsive, their continued residence in matter should be a testimony of their potential in this lifetime.

For each of us the preparing to die is unique. But what all such experiences have in common is the letting go of material ties. In order to have a smooth and relatively "painless" transition, we must release material fixation in the realm where we acquired it. Here in the earth we have the law of cause and effect at work, and here we can undo what we have done. We can work with those very laws, those memories and patterns which built our material affinities and release them much more easily than we will ever again find it possible.

All people of conscience have wrestled with their witnessing of pain and suffering. Some erroneously think that there is gain exclusively from enduring pain. Others of us think that suffering is noble because so many renowned historical figures have suffered. Suffering, in and of itself, is neither noble nor does it count for gain. The most beautiful music may have the note of middle C, but the note itself is not beautiful. By itself, a musical note is neither beautiful nor ugly; it only takes on quality or lack of quality by the context in which it is found. Our culture has developed such a reverence for suffering that we sometimes equate it with being blessed. In light of this broader understanding, where then is the growth in pain, where is the mercy in suffering, and how does it fit in with God's eternal plan?

As previously noted, it is vitally important that we release as much of our material fixation as possible before we move on to that realm we will call the borderland. This borderland is the first stage of reality we enter after death and the closest to material existence. Here in the borderland we begin to expand, to grow much, much larger. Helen Greaves in *Testimony of Light* describes this expansion as does Rudolf Steiner in *Theosophy*. If our condition were finite, we would see ourselves grow pro-

foundly larger in size. So too do our fixations grow and
cause us great stress if we have no way to satisfy them.
Our resulting anxieties grow so large that we eventually
inhabit them and are assaulted from all sides by them.
We can suffer beyond description as a result of improper
preparation. Any release of material ties in the earth before death is worth any price.

When we are ill or injured for a long while, we tend to
turn our attention from our vanity. At first we may be totally preoccupied with our pain, we may place our attention on our healing, we may invest our awareness in
our treatment, or we may even begin to develop a transcendent consciousness. In any case, turning away from
ourselves, from our own opinions, from the material
things of this world on which we have placed such a high
value is part, and a very important part, of our preparation for our transition. Some of us release our fixations
on a deeper level of our being, and we are fully prepared
to die. Yet others of us must draw out our transition in
such a way that we may be better prepared to move into
other realms. Illness and suffering play important roles
here, and in this context they are merciful experiences.
This discourse on suffering is not to imply that all must
agonize to be prepared to die, nor even that any must
suffer. It is, however, to show a way in which we release
that which holds us in the earth and to help us understand the transition process.

It cannot be stated too often that the spiritual perspective is inward and not outward. Once we leave the
physical realm we will view reality inwardly and not outwardly. All that we have placed inside ourselves will act
as a lens, a filter. All that we see will be seen through and
be distorted by these things we have stored within ourselves. This is why it is important to remove as much
clutter as possible so as not to obscure our reality. The
dimensions which immediately surround the earth have

been called the mental realms by both Cayce and Steiner. It is here we face, we inhabit, we experience what we have built into our minds as a result of our activities. It is in the mental realms where our minds embody our souls. In this reality we do not leave behind the attitudes we held in the earth but we inhabit them. We will discuss these realms in much greater detail in the next chapter, but this introduction is necessary to give us an idea of what we are preparing for.

Let us take an extreme example to better understand the transition process we are discussing here. In Judeo-Christian philosophy suicide is deeply frowned upon. Taking one's life is viewed as ranging from a sinful act to earning eternal damnation. So extreme are the Western taboos against suicide that we are compelled to look further at the act and its consequences. Long before one becomes suicidal, one begins to suffer. That which leads one to contemplate suicide may be physical or mental. Eventually, however, all suicidal motivation will be propelled from the emotions. One will suffer so greatly as to be willing to put an end to it at any cost. The suicide victim does not realize that what he or she perceived as the limits of ability to endure in materiality will become just the beginning of what must be borne as results of such an act of sacrifice. The conditions which lead to taking one's own life are so heavy to the soul, they are so built into the fabric of our minds, that death will not separate us one bit from them. This was illustrated many times in the Cayce discourses when he said that we not only take our attitudes with us into death, but we inhabit them. They will however become much, much larger in death, much harder to bear, with no way to set them aside easily. As a result we will suffer from those emotions which prompted our suicide ten, twenty, or even a hundred times more than if we endured the experience and grew from it as we had the potential to do. Rudolf Steiner in

Theosophy calls this experience "burning privation." If, for example, fear of loss becomes so overwhelming that it becomes that from which we hope suicide will set us free, that very attitude will appear infinitely larger after death. In material life we can deal with our fears and see them for what they are. In death we cannot always see beyond the emotion which envelops us and we are paralyzed by it. Let us not treat lightly the prospect of fear after death, for we can no more justify our fears before than after material death. A debilitating fear of loss has as much validity in death as it does in life except that the living do not see it that way. Piled upon this horror we have built to house us in that realm the Cayce discourses call the borderland are all of those other material fixations—those desires, fears, hates, and prejudices—that suicide victims take with them unadulterated into the realms which surround the earth. Of course there is growth and healing for those who have taken their own lives. But also there is suffering to so great an extent that Rudolf Steiner notes it leaves its mark upon us for several lifetimes thereafter.

Preparation is so vital a part of our transition that its lack will not only alter our path through the spiritual but will greatly influence our next incarnation. Many cultures allow for and even encourage the living to assist the dying. Such assistance is very important and helps those dying beyond anything that can be comprehended by those giving aid. Elisabeth Kübler-Ross has made a life work of counseling and studying the preparatory process in dying. In her book *On Death and Dying,* Kübler-Ross explores the five stages of dying as denial and isolation, anger, bargaining, depression, and finally acceptance. These five stages are recognizable signs of the internal adjustments being made to allow for a more orderly and helpful transition. Finally, in the end, we are so close to higher realities that the transition is just a short and effortless step. As we have said, illness and suffering are not required to prepare for this final step, but they are recognizable ways.

Dying is something we do gradually in spite of what may appear in materiality to be the opposite. The universe is perfect; there are no accidents, no coincidences, and "nothing happens by chance." (136-12) Whether our final step is the result of an accident, a crime, an illness, or just a quiet passing, nothing happens by chance. There are surely times where we have not sufficiently prepared for our transition, but this is by our own choice. Where we have denied others the opportunity to fulfill their potential we may choose to experience this ourselves. We may by our own choice become so shortsighted and reckless in our relationship with the Creative Forces that we forsake the opportunity to have an orderly awakening after that pivotal point we call death. One thing is certain; most of us are not equipped to understand if and when another is preparing for that change in consciousness we call death.

It is worth repeating that often in sleep and occasionally in meditation we make major adjustments, preparing a place where we will find ourselves after death. Cayce's dream discourses illustrated this point many times. With the assistance of God's ministers of grace, we begin to release those things in materiality to which we have so closely tied ourselves in life. We have focused our attention so narrowly and so intensely and for so long on material values, that it is far more difficult to release our fixation than we can realize. Simultaneously to releasing our material affections we build those things into our awareness which will immediately fill the resulting void. What we build to replace our material fixations are attitudes appropriate for better functioning in the spiritual realms. In the end, our transition is like stepping into our own thoughts where we have existed all along.

This is an inward step, so small, so natural; yet from a material perspective it is so abrupt, and so extreme. At the moment of change some of us are completely aware of what is happening, some of us only partly aware, and yet others totally unaware. Ultimately we meet and greet our own death with the same awareness and attention to detail we gave to our experiences in life.

Chapter 3

CHANGE CONTINUES

REGIONS, REALMS, AND PLANES

For those who believe that life is eternal, it is inevitable that they wrestle with the answers to the question of exactly what within us is eternal. On this single answer rests the beginning of all religious differences in the modern world. In *Tertium Organum,* P.D. Ouspensky writes, "All religions, all creeds begin by giving man one or another view of death. It is impossible to build any philosophy of life without one or another definition of death." In spite of death being such an inseparable part of life, Western culture has made an art form of avoiding any recognition of it. The subject of death has become to our society what the subject of sex was to the Victorian era. Further, Elisabeth Kübler-Ross in her book, *Death, the Final Stage of Growth,* notes, "It is difficult to accept death in this society because it is unfamiliar. In spite of the fact that it happens all of the time, we never see it." Inevitably, the way a society views death greatly influences the way it lives life.

To further understand death and its relationship to life, let us return to that pivotal point of change in our experience that we call death. There is a definite happening at that point we call death, the least of which is the falling away of the physical body. Our awareness, emotions, memories, likes, dislikes, desires, and fears all live on within us. We have tried to make a case thus far to illustrate that our consciousness more than our physical senses is what we are. We have used materiality but we are not material. When one writes, the printed word becomes the vehicle for transmitting the thoughts contained in what is written. Books are collections of printed thoughts which serve their purpose as excellent tools for communication. Books are portable, they are easy to transport, they need no other things or appliances to make them work, and they are digestible in whatever quantities the reader wishes. There are marvelous books, books that stimulate the intellect, awaken the imagination, and excite the soul. Yet books are not the thoughts; they are not the message but the carriers of the message. How much more are we not the vehicle but what is carried in the vehicle. We do not fail to exist when the vehicle is set aside. We are not nor have we ever been material; we just use materiality. All of our awareness, including our reasoning, memories, and emotional responses, exists beyond our physicalness. We access our awareness, but unlike our bodies it is not three-dimensional. So accustomed have we become to expressing our awareness in materiality that we find it difficult to view our consciousness as not material. Again, let us look at our own dreams to better illustrate the point under discussion. Dreams do not take place in materiality, and in spite of our utilizing material symbols we do not require materiality to dream. Dreaming is a subconscious process which takes place on another level of reality. We operate on this level of reality where dreams unfold even though we are aware of it only infrequently upon awakening. Does a symphony exist prior to being recorded on paper? If the most beautiful musical movement were never played, would it have never existed?

The composer draws upon the harmonies of the universe and transforms them in materiality into a magnificent symphonic work of art. Yet the transformation which takes place in mental realms is but an expression of what the Pythagoreans called "the music of the spheres," and when interpreted by skilled musicians, it is yet another expression once more removed from the original. Let us slow down here to view this unfolding expression of reality.

We begin with the harmonies of life as they interplay with each other in the higher realms of spirit. This we call the music of the spheres. As we move closer to the material realms, this song that all creation sings of its Creator is transformed in mental realms into what could be described as geometric harmonies. Steiner, Cayce, and Swedenborg described these harmonies as the vibrations resulting from the creative process. The infinite varieties of harmonies are the result of the infinite variety of creation. Harmonies in the mental are more structured, more confined, and by virtue of confinement less harmonious than in higher spiritual realms. When harmonies are finally expressed materially through the mind they are still less magnificent and less perfect than in the previous realm that is being expressed. As we move closer into materiality, the harmonies become less magnificent and essentially less creative. It must be borne in mind that this process does not pollute the harmonies; they are merely expressed in a more confined form, but ultimately they bear the imprint of those who finally channel this diminished music of the spheres. We are not to bring in these harmonies in a form not suitable for this realm. The highest contribution a composer, conductor, or musician can make to harmonies is to express them with the full force of the individuality of the one expressing them.

Finally, it is as unlikely that spirit ceases to exist if it is not expressed in mental realms as it is that mental expressions would be terminated if they were not expressed materially.

Now, we previously described that final step from material life as though stepping into one's own thought. This stepping into ourselves is an essential concept to absorb. Here, within ourselves is where we have always been from the beginning of our first creation. Of course when that first spark of life became us, we didn't have so much inside of ourselves as we do now, but we probably used what we had better. As we acquired experiences, they built upon each other and became an inseparable part of the fabric of our being. Nothing is more familiar or more hospitable to each of us than that which remains inside of ourselves. Everything we have ever been is within each of us, and if we face any surprises upon entering this reality, it is how oblivious we are in materiality to this.

Following our transition, we find that our motivations, values, and memories are essentially intact. For the soul who had lived what we would loosely call a "normally productive life" and prepared sufficiently for his or her transition, the only missing ingredient would be fear of separation. This fear of death is something originating in material realms and the very first of the fetters we choose to set aside after laying aside our physical bodies. In fact the loss of this fear of separation happens so naturally that we do not notice it unless we look to see what is missing. As we grow in those realms outside of the earth, we will leave behind certain attitudes which we "outgrow," and we will store other memories within other levels of ourselves for later use. If one would think of what was eaten for breakfast yesterday morning, the menu would probably be relatively easy to recall. It would require some thought though, as we do not necessarily keep information about our past breakfasts in the most accessible part of our memories. Now if one were to try to recall what was eaten for breakfast on an ordinary morning a year ago or even a month ago it would be very unusual to remember this. We would have eaten the food, remembered the experience for a relatively short period of time, and built its benefits into our bodies. Is what we eat important to us? It should be at the time we eat it. But as we assimilate the food by building blood, bone, nerve, and tissue, the result of what we ate becomes the predominant and more permanent reality. Our material experiences are to our soul what food is to our bodies. The memories, the relationships, the tastes of life are all carried over unadulterated in the first stage of death but as the digestive process continues they lose their prominence and our attention turns to other things.

One cannot objectively deliberate death or what exists beyond physical awareness without discussing the work of Dr. Raymond Moody. Dr. Moody has made a study of the experiences of people who were pronounced clinically dead and has drawn parallels where he has found experiences common to a variety of his subjects. It must be borne in mind, however, that all of Moody's subjects were products of twentieth-century culture; this is the least of what would affect their understanding of their own experiences. In his book *Life After Life*, Moody makes no claims to have found the literal face of death and liberally allows for common cultural values to shade his subjects' understanding of their death experiences. Nevertheless, Moody's work is a monumental success in inspiring countless people in all walks of life to begin to deal on an everyday basis with the prospect of their own immortality. Certainly Moody did not discover life after death. But the objective quality of his research combined with a methodical yet compelling presentation made his work a widespread contemporary masterpiece.

It is helpful to set forth a composite experience of the 150 individuals Moody studied as if they were under-gone by a single individual. Upon being pronounced dead the subject felt distress, followed by an uncomfort-able noise like a ringing or a buzzing. Then came a feeling of movement through a dark tunnel void of everything including any light, and this was followed by a state of emotional upheaval. As soon as the subject's thoughts were collected, there was a sense of timelessness and exceptional clarity. It was then perceived by the subject that one does indeed have a body, but it is of a different substance than one is accustomed to. At this point in the transition Moody's subject met others who were there to help. An all-loving being appeared whose compassion caused the subject to review the highlights of its life. At this point was a barrier separating "life and death." Here Dr. Moody's subject would decide to return to its body and resume material life.

Only experiences common to all were woven into those of the composite subject, and beyond these, per-sonal descriptions varied widely. The question will ulti-mately arise why and how did those who reached the barrier turn back, and the answer is threefold. First, their bodies were not beyond repair to resume being a practi-cal vehicle for their souls. Second, each felt compelling unfinished business. And third, force of will in each made return possible. One could ask the question, Why just these? What did they have that was so special? The answer is that this has probably happened thousands if not hundreds of thousands of times; of the very small group remembering the experience, only a smaller num-ber of people were willing to discuss it.

In the first stage following physical death we find our-selves in the realm which is made of and held together by the mental activity of life in materiality. Here in what we will call the nearest reaches of what Cayce termed the borderland, life is bigger than life. It is a narrow reality bordered on one side by a gradual density and on the other by a likewise gradual quickening or elevation. It is the state occupied by Dr. George Ritchie, Jr., which he describes in his book *My Life After Dying*. Further, it is the divide between life in the earth and life in the mental realms. This divide is in fact that part of the mental realm completely overlapped by the material realm. One can move into closer proximity to the earth and become so fixed by desire, as Ritchie observed, that one is unable to extricate oneself. One may move toward a quickening into finer realms or one may slide into one of the densest realms we call "outer darkness." Before we discuss this realm of the borderland and growth toward higher realms, let us first take a clear look at the two difficult options of either being fixed on materiality or of falling into outer darkness.

Many people who die surely do not do so willingly. For some, their deaths like their lives are rebellious and their minds are fixed on materiality. Before gaining a cognizance of what and where they are, they try to fly on the wings of their misguided values back into the density of materiality. One thing however is amiss; they are not material. As they go about trying to function, the newly discarnate entities do not understand why they cannot affect things the way they did before, why they cannot communicate with others; as a result, they are gripped by fear. The Cayce discourses contain much material on this state of confusion. Some think they have lost their minds, others think those around them have gone mad, and others adapt in this world of semireality. They do encounter objects that are manifestations of thought and have no way of separating them from those denser ones with which they cannot interact. This extreme edge of the mental realm is so close to materiality that it intertwines with it at every turn. The fact is that interaction with mental counterparts of material activity that exist in this stage of consciousness is so like materiality, so closely conjoined to the physical, that the lost soul cannot tell where one stops and the other begins. This confusion or blurring of divisions lends credence to the perception that the troubled soul is in the same physical state it held while embodied in the earth.

It is natural to ask why these souls who make their home at the edge of the borderland do not realize they have died and passed on to another reality. How often do dreamers realize they are dreaming even though activities are not what one would consider consistent with waking reality? The fact that the world works better for us when we do not occupy our illusions is not sufficient for us to set them aside as unreal. It is little wonder that we are not moved by the incongruity of reality in the borderland and accept it as very, very real. Here in this realm where mental meets material we most certainly have bodies, and they look very much as we do. For it is this self which has been expressed in materiality, and we have done all we can to conform our physical bodies to it. This self, this body is more essentially us than our physical bodies, more recognizable, and we do not think it at all unusual.

Some souls adjust to this confusion and as a consequence are tied to the earth for years. They derive their satisfaction by mingling with those forces, those energies which are given off from life in material realms. They live vicariously, as Dr. Ritchie described, in the emotions and mental activities of those in the earth. These emotions and mental activities have a spiritual expression, and while in this edge of the mental, they are like a musical note which has not yet joined the harmony of the symphony. The sound has been made and in that microsecond as it emanates from the instrument, before it joins the voice of the orchestra, it exists as the sound of potential harmony. Here is a parallel of forms we find in the borderland. The embodied emotions are like reflections which are traveling toward that off of which they will properly reflect. If one could mingle with such forms of potential, one could get the aroma of what they reflect but never the taste. In this state the forms are fully recognizable as that from which they emanate. Those souls who have trapped themselves in this region endlessly try to influence matters in the earth. Some are from time to time successful as they mix with thought patterns emanating from the earth plane and some are not. Some souls have even become self-destructive enough as to occupy or possess the body of a material human being who has by its own uncoordinated activities separated its mental from its physical forces. It may be hard to imagine that a soul who has finally made its transition from fear and pain, toward peace and growth, would choose to enter confusion and turmoil instead. But have we not seen those who sacrifice family values for greed? Have we not seen those who gave up the love of others for selfishness? We need only to look around us at those who make similar choices in their day-to-day relationships to understand that we do not always choose what is best for us regardless of the consequences.

God and all of creation personify patience and await our turning back to the road we began to travel after awakening in the borderland. To assist our return, there are countless ministers of mercy all about us in our existence in the borderland. These who would help us need only for us to will that help, for us to let go of our fixation on materiality; then they will set our shaky feet on the path we must follow. They will accomplish this by resonating in such a way that we will respond likewise, finding ourselves once again less dense and more firmly fixed in a higher form of reality in the farther reaches of the borderland. Helen Greaves in *Testimony of Light* dwells on these helpers throughout the book. For whether it is in the borderland or any region, we will exist in those dimensions to which we have a sympathetic resonance.

Let us now take a detour into a yet denser reality so we can better understand another of our options on awakening in the borderland. There are some of us who have lived our lives in such a way that we turned completely within ourselves. We blocked out all love, all warmth, all spirit from our daily doings; we created a void around ourselves. We chose to deny our responsibilities to others and to ourselves; we chose ourselves at all cost. Upon passing on, before we become conscious that we have entered the borderland, we swiftly move on to that realm to which our life choices in the earth resonate. This region is void of love, life, and light, void of all of those things we cast out from our lives in the earth. The region in which we find ourselves is approximately our wish come true. We are truly alone, with ourselves, within ourselves; it is pain beyond pain for us. Edgar Cayce described this region of void as "outer darkness." The name of this dimension describes it very accurately, as we find no love, hope, friendship, kindness, benevolence, or any of what we have come to know as human qualities. Instead there is nothing but ourselves, and it is unbearable. In the absence of that which we term fruits of the spirit— truth, love, patience, gentleness, kindness, long-suffering, and brotherly love—we fill the void with an irrational and unbelievable amount of pain and fear. It is so dark in the realm of outer darkness that the dark hurts and panic grips us without our knowing why. Like our material universe, outer darkness seems endless and without any meaningful boundaries. There is nowhere we can go to escape the agony and horror which fills almost every part of our being, and the desire to flee consumes us. The farther and faster we travel through this realm the greater the feeling that it is endless. Even outer darkness has degrees, and it is darker and denser at the center than at its outer fringes. Helen Greaves describes these degrees as hells. Likewise, this is the hell described by Emanuel Swedenborg in *Heaven and Its Wonders and Hell from Things Heard and Seen.* The closer we are to the outer edges, the more interaction there is with others in the realm, while the closer to the center we find ourselves, the darker and more painful we find the solitude. One in outer darkness cannot move toward the center or edges by force of one's own motion. The center or edges are levels of reality and are not linear. One cannot travel across this dimension; one must grow through the levels of this realm.

Outer darkness is not one of those realms which must be overcome in stages, although we can choose that method of growth. One may find oneself on a particular level after death that most closely corresponds to one's activity and the degree of absence of those fruits of the spirit in one's life, and there is no need to experience other levels here. No level of outer darkness is without pain and fear, but, as we have noted, the very center is the most agonizing. In the reality we call outer darkness we have very little memory of our earthly lives. We remember little if anything of our earthly relationships, and we are so absorbed in pain and fear that our suffering exacts every last ounce of our attention.

This lower region of outer darkness is not a punishment. It is a region which operates lawfully for the benefit of those agonized souls. This region is not a realm which was created for any soul to experience, but one which came about as a consequence of the negative activity of souls in creation. So great has been the desire for self, so monumental across time and space has been the selfishness of some of God's creatures that this realm is the creation or manifestation of their own collective activities. Outer darkness and the reality with which it is associated were created and are held in place by collective self-interest.

As noted previously, universal law is perfect and works for the benefit of all, all of the time. An excellent example of the Law of Grace is that no evil, no negativity, no matter how single or collective in nature, exists without a way of redemption being simultaneously imprinted by the Creative Forces throughout its fiber. Nowhere else is it so obvious than in the realm of outer darkness because no one need remain here beyond one's own will to do so. We might conjecture that no one wishes to suffer such misery but that simply is not so. We constantly do things in the earth that cause us difficulty, unhappiness, pain, and illness. We do not wish to suffer the discomfort of our actions, but this does not keep us from those activities. In the earth as in spiritual realms, until we turn our attention from ourselves, we cannot in any way change our estate.

What would one dwelling in outer darkness look like? In *Witness from Beyond,* Ruth Mattson Taylor describes some of this region, and her description is not unlike that of Helen Greaves's, Emanuel Swedenborg's, and Rudolf Steiner's. Appearance varies with whomever is beholding it. To those who occupy the same level of outer darkness, each would appear to the other very much the way he or she did in the earth. To those on higher levels of reality, those who dwell in outer darkness would appear sickly and deformed. To those who inhabit the highest realms of reality, those who occupy outer darkness would appear as monsters, barely alive embodiments of those horrible emotions they exude. How would outer darkness appear to its occupants? Those toward the center, who have no contact with any other creatures, would see outer darkness as the blackest black. Even the sight of such blackness would cause pain and panic throughout the being of its inhabitants. As one moved closer to the edges, outer darkness would appear as a gray, colorless area, in a half-dark, half-light surrounding; thick with fog. Terrible odors would reek from the vaporous fog; inhabitants would look angry and pained, dirty, shabbily clothed, and menacing. Dwellings would appear equally poor and run down in the nearest edges of outer darkness; and as in other levels, this reality would seem to be without end. No source for the half light which prevailed everywhere would be apparent, and the fog would grow thicker at times. The thicker the fog appeared to be, the greater the stench. It would seem as if the fog were the aroma of evil as its manifestation rose into spiritual reality. As one moved toward the center, gradually the images would become more pronounced, more disgusting, and fearful until utter darkness and panic prevailed. The inhabitants of outer darkness would not act very differently than they did in the earth while they were preparing a place here for themselves, and those occupants who had contact with others would be highly combative. There are no alliances among the occupants of outer darkness; tormenting one another would be the natural state of relationships.

Ruth Mattson Taylor in *Witness from Beyond* describes those beings in outer darkness, who may be called spirits that attach themselves, so to speak, to the occupants. They cannot be seen nor are the occupants aware of them. They interact with the occupants not through their thoughts but through their affections. Likewise, these spirits are those who transform the collective selfishness of all souls into the realm of outer darkness. As the keepers of outer darkness, these spirits influence the affections of all who will to do evil and constantly keep the flow of evil from souls to realms and from realms to souls.

No less is the influence of angels of mercy in outer darkness, as seen by Emanuel Swedenborg, who likewise work on the affections of the miserable and tormented souls. The angels are not so close by in the depths of outer darkness as the spirit keepers, but their influence is just as great if not greater. The goal of the angels in outer darkness is to turn the attention of its occupants away from themselves. Angels do not spend all of their time in the depths of outer darkness for they must periodically raise their awareness for revitalization and sustenance. As we move farther toward the edges of outer darkness, there are those angels and more evolved souls who have taken as their mission to work with the souls trapped in outer darkness. The closer one moves toward the edges of outer darkness, the more practical it becomes to work through the thoughts of the occupants; at the very edges there is actual discourse between the occupants and ministers of mercy. Those who work with the thoughts of the souls in outer darkness must slow themselves down considerably, but not nearly as much as those who actually converse with the tormented souls. The evolved souls and other ministers of mercy work with those in outer darkness; their mission is ultimately to elevate these tormented souls to the realms of the borderland. Here in the borderland are those ministers who will keep their charge and help the souls to yet higher realms.

Now, how do these ministers of mercy appear to the occupants of outer darkness? When they do appear to the occupants, they do so first as only a presence and then as shadows. Finally, because of the extreme self-occupation of the souls trapped in outer darkness, when the ministers converse with them, they appear to be beings in whom they have no interest and about whom they have a great deal of suspicion. It is, however, through these angels of mercy that God keeps a balance in outer darkness and does not let any soul be tormented beyond what it could bear.

The occupants in outer darkness are there for various lengths of time. It is peculiar to discuss length of residence by a measure which does not exist in that dimension. For most of us it is very difficult to relate to a timeless condition, so the use of finite terms helps us to better understand. Some residents feel they have been in outer darkness for weeks or months, others for eons. No doubt all are correct in their assessment of length of time spent in this realm. In a reality of pain and torment, even a moment can seem like an eternity and there is no way to judge length of stay until after one has long departed. Doubtless some souls have occupied outer darkness for what we would measure as hundreds, even thousands of years. But it is more likely that most stay for a considerably shorter period. It is not possible for souls to be forever confined to outer darkness, since in such a case there would be no hope of redemption. Further, Swedenborg in *Heaven and Its Wonders and Hell from Things Heard and Seen* noted that it is God who keeps the balance in the realm of outer darkness so that all things would not be destroyed. Again, outer darkness is not a punishment, rather it is the ultimate manifestation of our own undoing, and He who is Mercy would never abandon us to such spiritual agony.

Outer darkness seems such a horrible place that one would wonder how such a place can exist. If God is the God of love, then how can He allow such a place to exist and how can we who are sparks of God create and keep in place such realms? For an answer let us look only at the past few days of our lives. Were we selfish? Did we benefit at the expense of anyone else? Was our sense of our own importance elevated? Let us go even further to magnify the behavior we are asking about. Did we give to others of our time, of our supply, not of our excess but of our substance? Did we help someone, not just at the price of inconvenience but at a real cost to ourselves? Did we fail to do all we could because we wouldn't try for fear of the appearance of failure? These flaws will not consign us to outer darkness. But the roots of these attitudes are found firmly planted in the lowest realms of life. As we magnify these attitudes we come closer and closer in the earth to the true meaning of outer darkness and bring pain to our souls beyond our conscious realization. As we block the light of God from our lives we approximate outer darkness, to the extent of the shadow our selfishness casts on our own unfolding reality.

Let us return our attention to the realm that we call the borderland. The borderland is the outer edge of the mental realms overlapping materiality. All that we experience in materiality is manifest in its purity in the mental realms. When one is in any of the mental realms, reality seems so much purer, so much more real. One arriving here would become aware that there has definitely been a change, an awakening. What we would perceive as our senses in this realm would seem infinitely sharper, and we would be much more sensitive. All that is material is but an expression of what is manifest in the mental realms. So here we find ourselves with the authentic original and not the copy. As we look around and absorb our surroundings, we feel as though we have just emerged from a haze. We do not see anything we did not see on earth and everything is quite familiar. There are those around us that we know. Some may have been friends or relatives who passed on before us, and others may be souls not incarnate with us with whom we shared a genuine connection. We do not notice all of the souls around us but just those with whom we have sympathy or shared experience.

It may be difficult to grasp having many souls around us yet seeing just a few. So let us relate that to earthly experiences. There is a puzzle in which the reader is to find familiar shapes in the design of the picture. One popular such game is called "Where Is Waldo?" If we are told what to look for, we find more shapes than if we must find them without first knowing they are there. Now, let us try to imagine a picture in which one must identify some shapes that we are told are built into the design, some which we are not told about, and some shapes the player has never before seen or heard of. It is likely that the player will do well on the first part, not so well on the second, and will do nothing at all on the third. The shapes we were unable to identify just seem like part of the design and as such do not exist apart from that pattern. This in effect is what the newly arrived soul experiences—the souls with whom they do not have shared sympathy seem like part of the overall pattern of the realm and not individual souls.

We notice that sleeping and waking seem to be faculties still with us as Ruth Mattson Taylor noted. We feel that we have just wakened, and we go through periods of what appear to us to be states of awake and asleep. Certainly we do not need sleep outside of the earth. But we are accustomed to periods of rest and seize the opportunity when first entering the mental realms. Gradually this cycle of sleep and work leaves us. But we do find periods of refreshment akin to rest. We have a major adjustment to make and all of those we meet in the borderland are there to help us. In every realm that we find ourselves in between lives, there are those who are resident in those dimensions, except for the borderland. This state of reality is unique in that it is a transient state for all who inhabit it. There are those souls and beings who choose to work for the betterment of souls in the borderland, but they are still visitors and not residents there.

In the borderland is where we review in detail the life

in the earth just lived. We see our lives with a clarity obscured from us when we were in the earth. We see the potential, the ultimate possibilities of all of the choices we didn't make. Although this is an emotional experience, Steiner notes that we are protected by those beings around us from immersion in our own emotions and becoming lost. There is not one review, but several; each exacts yet another focus. Although we are free from the fetters of time and space, we still take this review process gradually so that we are not overcome and immobilized. Part and parcel to this review, a healing takes place. As the scars left on the mind become evident, a healing takes place so that the soul will be able to move on. Now we take note of great beings of light for the first time, and we are struck by how we recognize them. There is total familiarity and the realization of their always having been with us, whether before, during, or after our earth life.

As we move further from the review process, we become more fixed in the mental realms. We leave the mental-material overlap and move more into that part of the mental which we will now call the First Region of reality after death. Rudolf Steiner in *Theosophy* discussed at great lengths successive realms he called the First Region, Second Region, and so forth. Because we draw so heavily on Steiner's work in this chapter, we will use the same terminology as he did. Now, we are fully invested in reality beyond physical materiality, and those periods of rest in which we approximate sleep are behind us. We will from here and throughout the spiritual realms now experience ceaseless activity, since life, like the spirit which it animates, is continuous. This region is ruled by those things which comprise such emotions as our urges, passions, sensual love, and all that is connected with them. Here in the First Region we begin to deal with our unfinished emotional business left from our past incarnation. Those who lived by and were ruled mostly by their emotions will have more difficulty in this realm than those who were not. Those who are still fixated on earthly desires will feel an expansion of those yearnings and will suffer by virtue of the inability to satisfy them directly. In any event, the soul will not move on until all of its material fixation is laid aside. Some of the desires, Steiner notes, will be purged permanently and others will be left aside in "safe keeping" to be dealt with at a more appropriate time.

This laying aside is a concept which may be alien to some, because we think of spiritual progression as an overcoming rather than a continuous experience. In the First Region, as in others, we deal with those parts of ourselves which are ruled by forces which emanate through that realm. We are not required to deal successfully with all of those things; we will not pass this way only once, so we can set aside what can better be dealt with elsewhere and return later to reclaim it. We may not pass from the First Region carrying our emotional ties to materiality; so we will deal with what we can and will move on. We cannot choose to set aside that which we are able to successfully deal with, just because the challenges are difficult, for our soul forces united with this region will not permit us to delude ourselves in such a way. Here in the First Region we live in communities with those with whom we share a like sympathy.

Helen Greaves, Ruth Montgomery, Edgar Cayce, Rudolf Steiner, Emanuel Swedenborg, and Ruth Mattson Taylor all discuss these groups, communities, or societies at great length. We share relationships with souls with whom we have done so throughout our travels through reality. There are those in every realm who are part of our soul group, those with whom we have shared experiences, and those who will remain our soul family throughout our experiences. On each level of reality

there are those who are resident in that dimension. Such
entities, who are not transient to the level in which we
find ourselves, are as unaware of our presence as we are
of theirs. Similarly there are countless life forms passing
through the material dimension of which we are largely
unaware. We each travel different paths, and it may not
be in the best interests of either of us to share relationships in the process. The mental regions are ones influ-
enced by sympathy and as such we relate only to that
with which we harmonize. Relationships, affinity, values,
experiences, enlightenment all resonate throughout
material and spiritual realms, and we are drawn together
by the harmonious forces of sympathy. It is this very
force of sympathy by which we are impelled beyond the
material earth to the very regions we have prepared for
ourselves.

Our communities in the First Region appear to us
much the same as they did in the earth. But they appear
slightly different to each inhabitant. As we grow in a region, its appearance changes, but this is so gradual it
goes largely unnoticed. All experiences are for learning;
here we deal largely with our choices in our most recent
earth incarnation. We do not merely deal with observation but we actually inhabit the experience in all of its
potential. This may be difficult to understand, so let us
again explain by illustration. In the earth we may have
had an experience of helping another to grow. This
choice may have caused us difficulty to a varying degree
and may have opened the door to countless choices
along our journey. The experience could have been com-
plicated and spread over a long period of time. In the
First Region we may experience the glory of the growing
of fields of magnificently beautiful flowers. Such flowers
would not only be attractive in appearance but beautiful
beyond explanation to our soul. We may experience the
radiance, the peace, the glorious symphony of creation

at play in the fields and then we may find ourselves the keeper of these fields. The flowers whose beauty we now experience on every level find their growth and nourishment at our hand. We are the gardeners of the fields, the symphonic conductors of beauty; we share an exclusive relationship with what they represent. Likewise we deal with our not so glorious choices by having the opportunity to be changed by their true essence.

For those who chose to experience materiality more passively, the First Region is more difficult than for those who made inappropriate choices. As much can be learned from unsuitable choices as from correct ones; but nothing can be learned from making no choice. If we lived a life of indifference in the earth, Steiner notes that in the First Region we experience a helpless and useless state of being where we cannot participate in life around us. We have a burning desire to associate, to experience but are not guided by impelling forces that draw us into such experiences. We experience our own indifference and then see the possibilities all around us of our choices. The desire to participate in any of our possible choices wells up inside of us, because we see the full potential of those options never taken. We need not see the earthly potential of the choices not made, but the emotional, mental, and spiritual possibilities. For a while or what may seem like a thousand years we find our experience very difficult. Then finally, when we have fully experienced our indifference, we begin to set it aside to be combated after we have gained more protective light for the task.

As we deal with our earthly experiences good and bad, unfolding in their full potential, we glean the best and overcome or set aside the worst. All with whom we associate help us in our relationships to reality. We meet those with whom we feel close and others with whom we feel distant. Our clarity of vision and our relationships are in proportion to our affection; we have only the most limited use of the laws of cause and effect at this time. Life here is accented by the fact that we cannot change one bit our relationships with others. The lack of the full force of cause and effect seems so natural that we do not question it or even lament its absence. As in the earth, we are surrounded by angels and other spirits. But their presence is somewhat more discernible to the senses of this dimension. Swedenborg and Steiner agree that as we rise into finer dimensions, those permeating from yet higher dimensions are more apparent to us. We all work together to experience the spiritual potential of our activities and are protected, guided, and healed by the angels of mercy.

From the First Region we take trips, as described by Helen Greaves, into higher dimensions and return again to use those experiences in our communities. This is not so unusual when one acknowledges that the same things are experienced in our sleep state in the earth. Frequently we move out of our earthly bodies in sleep and travel to spiritual realms. This is accomplished under the guidance and protection of souls and spirits who have taken this as their ministry. The only difference is that after death, we do not sleep and we vividly recall the experience of having traveled to another dimension. Greaves notes that, when appropriate, those who minister always to us come to us; they change their own vibrations to be sympathetic with the realm to which we are to travel. Like two tuning forks, we are drawn to their resonance and eventually vibrate at the same rate. This process transports us to that realm with which we have been helped to develop a sympathy, where we are ultimately instructed and refreshed. When our experience is complete we return to the First Region where we once again resonate to this dimension. Such a form of travel is not limited to the First Region and in fact exists in almost all dimensions of reality. It may seem hard to conceive of, but before we leave we expand to fill out all of the First Region. Each individual in the region occupies the same time and space but interacts only in accord to those with whom each has had a relationship.

Passing on from one region to another is not as traumatic as the exit from the physical earth. It is not as outwardly abrupt nor are we as likely to become as fixed in these regions as we did in materiality. When our experiences in the First Region are complete we leave behind those karmic memories we will again reclaim and move to the Second. Here we now find ourselves in a balanced state of sympathy and antipathy. In such a balanced state we no longer are gripped by regrets of unfulfilled potential and are much more objective in our experiences. Here in the Second Region we are also divided into communities but are as unaware of those outside of our community as we were in the First Region. Swedenborg mentioned that those who led indifferent lives in the earth are still relatively isolated from others; but their need for being part of the soul family is no longer as burning as it may have been in the First Region, nor does it last as long. Here, in this region, sympathy and antipathy are general laws and do not attach themselves to things as they do in the earth, the lower planes, or the First Region. Because of this, emotions triggered by situations and things pass very quickly. We have now begun to move away from the relationship of experiences and the emotions they arouse, and likewise we have begun to deal with creation in a more balanced fashion. Here in the Second Region we begin to appear much younger if we lived past middle age in the earth. This is not a physical youth but an internal youth. If we were to appear to others in materiality at this time we would project that image we had at the height of our physical vitality. The further we move through the regions outward from materiality, the younger and more vital we appear internally. We are illumined by those great ministers of mercy, and we receive life, light, and wisdom through this irradiation. In this region we are much more aware than ever before of those influences which work upon us; life becomes much more instructive for us. We still deal largely with our earth choices and potentials, but because sympathy and antipathy are in balance, we do so much more objectively.

It is not so outrageous to wonder about our appearance in the other regions outside of the earth. In the First Region we would have an appearance remarkably similar to the one we had in the earth, but far less dense. We would not only look more like ourselves than we did in the earth but we would be almost transparent at times. In the Second Region we would leave behind even this transparent density of the First Region and would appear to others in the true nature of our attitudes and experiences. Remember that in materiality we often see others, especially our loved ones with "eyes" that no one else uses. We see with a combination of our spiritual and physical senses and the result is a far clearer image although not physically accurate. Often we say those that we know do not look much like their photographs or that it is a bad picture. The physical camera does not take into account the essence of its subject, therefore it can only capture the grossest material reflection of a person. No one is what he or she looks like in a photograph, but this becomes evident only to those who have a relationship with the subject. We have all heard that "love is blind"; but far from myopic, love is more revealing about the true appearance of another person. Consequently, the further we move from material manifestation the more accurate are the images we project and observe. However, when we are perceived by others in any region, including physical earth, we take on an appearance to them suitable to that realm. We can only be observed in any realm with the senses of that realm; therefore, appearance is what is beheld and essence is what is reflected.

Rudolf Steiner noted that in the Second Region we interact more with spirits, souls, and angels from higher realms, and our travels to other dimensions continue at the same rate as they did in the First Region. Like before, our travels are to give us that which we need to better grow in the Second Region as we continue to work with the elevation and true nature of our lives just lived in the earth. We feel just as close to those in our communities as we did in the First Region and we find that we possess a striking familiarity with all of those we contact.

All activity in the Second Region is mental and we are present by force of our mental energy. We can easily find ourselves anywhere we wish just by thought and can even be in more than one place at a time. Omnipresence is a concept we find difficult to relate to in materiality, but it is far more natural a state in other regions. We have shadows of omnipresence in the earth, where we can be several places by force of our influence. We are aware of how mechanical communication devices can lend an aura of omnipresence to our being in the earth, but these are only the poorest reflections of the true omnipresence which is a normal attribute in other regions ruled by mental or spiritual energy. Helen Greaves wrote that in the Second Region we have just to think of something and it is reality. However, we cannot change things as they exist; we can only experience them. Essentially reality works on us rather than us on it, and although we can move into any or all aspects of reality, we cannot in any way modify what we experience.

The pattern is the same; as we grow in experience, we expand to fill more and more of the region we occupy, until we embody it all. Nonetheless, we do not crowd out the countless others who occupy the same time and space as we do, for we have left time and space far behind us in the earth. When leaving the Second Region we leave behind those illusions created by our mental activities in the earth. But by contrast with the First Region, we do not return to pick up anything left behind in this realm. Anything of a karmic nature is left in the First Region, and all that we shed thereafter is totally discarded.

Before going any further we would explain our method of perception in the many realms through which we travel. When we say "we see," this does not mean we have eyes in a physical sense as we do in the earth. When we say "we hear," this likewise does not mean we have ears to hear with. We perceive with our transcendent senses, and sight, hearing, smell, taste, and touch have their nonmaterial counterparts. In the earth, we develop certain senses above the others, but outside of the earth they are all balanced. Outside of the earth our "sight" helps us to identify things while our "hearing" enables us to understand them by their resonance. Our "taste" helps us to measure what we comprehend against what we ourselves are, and our "smell" helps us to absorb and make a part of ourselves all that we experience. Lastly, our sense of "touch" helps us to know the resistance and thus relative limits of what we encounter.

We use these same nonphysical senses even in the earth but are generally inattentive to them. If we close our eyes, we can still imagine images which may be sharper and clearer than we see with our physical eyes. If we think of a catchy tune, we can hear it inside of us for hours and even days, but we do not use our ears for this. When we fear or have great anxiety, we often hold our breath for a moment, almost as an automatic response, so we will not make that part of our experience a permanent part of ourselves. When we are satisfied, do we not breathe a deep sigh? Do we not taste fear, triumph, trial, and their kin? We find these pleasing or not by our taste or by measuring them against what we ourselves are. Lastly, we view reality by its limits. Nothing so qualifies the limits of anything as does its resistance to us. As children we learn we cannot walk through objects, that hard or dense things must be treated differently than soft or less dense ones. Do we not feel our way around situations by learning their boundaries? We could go on and on, but the point has been made that we can perceive outside the earth with senses corresponding to those we use in the earth; we even use these etheric senses in the earth alongside of our physical senses.

The Third Region is that from which our desires emanated and one in which Rudolf Steiner notes we experience all of our earthly wishes. This includes our ambitions, our yearnings, our hopes, and all else connected with them. Here in this realm we work with the unfoldment of all we had aspired to in the earth and see these aspirations blossom in their full purity. We are relatively unaffected emotionally, because we have left such a capacity behind in the First Region. We experience not what we had aspired to, but rather the combination of our earthly motivation and our expectation, raised to their ultimate expression. Those who were particularly religious in the earth spend the longest time or experience more in the Third Region than others, as also do those with very strong faith. Those whose lives were more mental in their attitudes spend far less time in this region than those who were not. As in other realms, we live in community in the Third Region and work together as well as with the angelic kingdom as described by Emanuel Swedenborg. Also, we cannot change what we experience in the Third Region. We travel out of this region from time to time as in the others which preceded it. There are striking similarities between the First, Second, and Third Regions. One deals with the mental, another the emotional, and another with the aspirations.

The Fourth Region is the region of attraction and repulsion. When passing through this region we have the opportunity to deal with our earthly likes, dislikes, and our attachment to them. Steiner notes that here, in the Fourth Region, growing souls complete purging themselves of remaining earthly attachments before moving on. Community is especially important because of the help and support it can give in the overcoming of those last great material weights we still carry. Because we are digging deep into our consciousness, this process can make for a difficult journey. Both the angels of grace and mercy are present in abundance to protect us from being overcome by more than we can deal with. Most of all this region is especially difficult for those who died because of suicide. Although the karmic memories were left in the First Region, the soul passing through this region has not yet sufficiently shed its attachments to material conditions. The burden of the suicide victim, unlike other souls, is especially great at this time, and its antipathy is magnified many times. Here is where such a soul will eventually deal with its revulsion and will not move on until that process is complete.

It is difficult to describe what we look like in this realm of the Fourth Region except by three-dimensional concepts. First of all we are youthful and vibrant. Much of our physical imperfection is gone; if we would perceive the features of our image, they would appear totally symmetrical. Our dwelling place, which would be a product of our mental processes, would likewise be orderly and well balanced. To those about us we would appear honest, relatively innocent, and all around us would wish to be protective of us. Steiner makes note that those in this region who are recovering from suicide appear much

darker in color than the others, not as well formed; they
live in dwellings that appear to be older and in need of
repair. Most souls in the Fourth Region have a keen sense
of self, but this identity is far more objective than sub-
jective.

As in other realms we are not resident but transient in
the Fourth Region, and we also take leave of this region
occasionally to visit others. We never travel alone but are
guided and helped by spirit guides in our journeys.
When visiting another realm we take on the form of that
realm, or we could not exist fully within it. As an example, if we were to visit the physical earth we would
probably go as far as what we earlier called the outer
fringes of the borderland. Here we would take on the
form we had just after leaving material life, only it would
be modified by our interior changes which have since
taken place. We would probably look younger, healthier,
more vibrant, and remarkably like we would have looked
under such conditions in a physical body. Our exteriors
would be comprised of finer matter which we have conformed to our interior reflection. One of the functions of
our guardian would be to adjust our vibratory patterns
so that we could attract and take on the matter of the
borderland. The adjustment would come about by our
guardian's establishing and drawing us into a sympathetic resonance to this region as described by Helen
Greaves in her work. The same process holds true when
we visit any realm in which we are not currently anchored.

As in the Second and Third Realms, we discard what
we leave behind in the Fourth Region without returning
to reclaim any of it. It cannot be repeated frequently
enough that our transition from one level of reality to
another is gradual and without the trauma we may have
suffered in leaving the earth. The reason separation from
the earth is so traumatic is because of our fixation re-

sulting from such an extremely narrow focus.

In the Fifth Region we find that our sympathy with our community and all of those who inhabit it reaches its highest point. Here, Steiner notes, one grows from a stage similar to attachment to earthly things for their sensory values to attachment to them because they are representative here of God and life in higher realms. We work largely on our sympathy here, so that before we leave it will resonate to all here that is representative of what is holy. From the Fifth Region we begin to perceive life being resonated and held together by the harmonies which the Pythagoreans called the Music of the Spheres. This becomes the first region since leaving the material earth where we begin to appreciate the creative force of harmonies. At first we are overwhelmed by the magnificence of the harmonies, the awesomeness of the "music"; then when we gradually overcome our initial wonder, we begin to work with the harmonies. As part of our learning process we witness symphonies of life unlike anything we could ever have imagined. With the help of our more experienced fellow souls as well as the ministers of grace, we mix with the harmonies; we vibrate to their resonance and become almost as one with them. We are not allowed to go too deeply into mixing with the "music" because we are not yet ready to do so. If we were not kept toward the outer edges of the harmonies, we would risk becoming spiritually paralyzed and being permanently lost at this stage of our growth. All reality is the result of the combined activity of seemingly countless sources, acting together, transforming spirit to give it form. In this way manifest spirit can be said to have compound form, which we do not even begin to understand until we blend with the musical harmonies where we find the combined creative process, or compounding, in a much more primal state of existence. Subsequently, the benefit gained from our experience with the harmonies is that we learn through experience more of how compound reality is manifest. The experience in this region is to move ever closer to our awareness of oneness with our surroundings and to renew this attribute within ourselves. As in the other regions discussed, we cannot cause anything to happen to ourselves or our surroundings. We are changed as is our relationship with our surroundings by being acted upon by the realm and all whom we encounter there.

In the Sixth Region we find those impulses which move us into material action. Void of those things which were acquired in and tied us to the earth, we are able to use this impulse in truly creative fashion. Steiner observed that former artists, musicians, poets, and scientists are especially at home in the Sixth Region where they learn how to move their creative focus from materiality to spirituality. In the Sixth Region we are active, but active only with experience. Our experience is transforming but has no external effect. Consequently, we still cannot change anything we find about us, because we left cause and effect a long, long way behind. From here on we are less likely to visit lower regions or the physical earth. In the Sixth Region we have now moved so far from physical manifestation that we have little interest in the affairs of the earth. We have learned by experience in all of the realms since leaving the earth, but here is where we learn of the blessings of continuous activity for God's sake.

In the Seventh Region where we complete the first stage of growth after a material life lived in the earth, we finally become free of all earthly impulses. Here we find ourselves in a community with all of those who are on the same level as ourselves. We find ourselves in surroundings which are entirely of our own true nature. There are no emblems of materiality here nor are there any resemblances between the forces we encounter and materiality. Here in this final level of growth in this first series of regions, we no longer have any desire to visit the earth nor any preceding realm through which we have traveled. When we first arrived in the Seventh Region we were certain that we had reached our eternal home. So in tune were we with it that there was not even a hint of internal conflict. We could not conceive of any higher order of life than here, from where we were certain the Music of the Spheres originated. Gradually we learn that there are higher realms of life, and we are in yet another stage of growth.

After the Seventh Region we will reverse the flow to which we have grown accustomed. Instead of releasing, we will begin acquiring. In the first six regions we had to release our fixations to become refreshed and allow for the influx of spiritual gifts. Now, as Swedenborg observed, we will experience influx continually. Here in the Seventh Region we are prepared for such a condition by the harmonies and every energy which embraces us. We are modified so that we may again receive internal energies more continually. We no longer live in the result of our earthly activities. We live in a region made up of that which is sympathetic to our soul essence.

When we have been sufficiently prepared, we leave the entire set of regions in which we released our earthly ties. Rudolf Steiner called the first group of seven regions the Soul Land and the next seven regions the Spirit Land. The next seven regions are made up of the same substance of which thought consists. This is not thought as we had in the material body but a truer, unadulterated, and primal thought. In the Spirit Land there is ceaseless creating which takes place. Rest, immobility, and stillness do not exist in these regions, nor are they necessary. In these regions are found the archetypes which are creative beings and the builders of all that comes into being in the material and soul realms. They draw upon spirit from yet higher realms and transform it into a seemingly endless variety of forms which take shape in other realms. Shapes of infinite variety flow from the archetypes and no sooner does one end than a completely different one begins. The archetypes work together in unison and share a very close relationship. They cannot operate alone and even though each appears to be creating separately, the archetypes are totally dependent one on the other.

Steiner wrote that each archetype is visible to the senses of the realm in which it resides and it emits a sound as it creates. The sound of each archetype mixes with the sounds of the others, as they interact, expressing themselves in a variety of harmonies and spiritual music. The melodies and rhythms which result are not only the byproduct of creation but they are creative in themselves. All that is seen here can be heard as well. The lights and colors correspond to the harmonies and melodies which likewise correspond to the creative process. All is creative, all is in motion, visible, audible, and all can be perceived by the senses of that realm. The Spirit Land is one of brilliant lights, colors, harmonies, and melodies, all in concert with one another.

As we enter the regions of the Spirit Land we lose ourselves in the life of these realms. We lose our sense of personal identity, but not our individuality, and take on the characteristics of each of the Spirit Regions we pass through. Our being is permeated with the life in each sphere, and we will use as faculties in our next earthly incarnation what we experience here. Unlike the regions of the Soul Land, here we do not work on or even experience ourselves. We are however worked on by the forces of each region, and we experience the essence of each dimension in which we find ourselves.

In the First Region of the Spirit Land we are surrounded by archetypes of material things. From this realm matter is transformed from the mental to the material. There is life and activity everywhere in this, the lowest region of the Spirit Land. Here in the First Region all activity is heard as music and all of the music blends together in magnificent harmonies. The physical forms created here appear more as a presence than as fixed. Gradually the presence is seen as a distortion and finally as dark outlines against the colors which emanate from the harmonies.

Steiner commented that what is considered to be just thoughts in lower realms become reality in this First Region. Here we move among the thoughts and we experience their essence. The thoughts have form, and as we pass through them we experience the full potential of each one. We now have the opportunity to see how reality arises in the earth and how our thoughts work upon the fabric of reality. Although we live in community, we no longer have a sense of personality. We have a much greater sense of membership than we do of self. We feel a growing unity with our community, our society, and the entire region. We feel an inseparable union with the archetypes, all that they transform into reality, and one with the primordial spirit. Those in the earth who eventually feel one with nature and one with the material region draw this awareness from the First Region of the Spirit Land. It is in this First Region we have the opportunity to see and experience our thoughts as ultimate reality.

In the earth we experience thought on a continuum of time and space. This means that our experience takes place gradually and in measured amounts. In this First Region of the Spirit Land we experience primal creative thought in its fullest sense from origin through manifestation.

In the earth what sets clairvoyants apart from others is their ability to perceive and understand potentials which arise from thought. From this First Region and onward we experience and are fully aware of just such potential.

As in the regions of the Soul Land, there are those in the Spirit Land who are permanent residents in each realm we pass through. As we work in each region we are as unaware of their presence as they are of ours. Those souls that we commune with in each region are part of our eternal family with whom we have always been connected. Many souls that we encounter are those we have lived with in most of our earthly incarnations, while more yet we have moved with through successive realms, and many are members of our soul family with whom we have never lost touch throughout creation.

In the Second Region of the Spirit Land we find the archetypes of life. Steiner noted that these archetypes transform thought matter into living things in the earth. Here in this region we see the relationship of life in the human family and all other living creatures. We develop an appreciation and respect for the oneness of all life and how any one life affects all other life. Unity takes on a whole new meaning for us in the Second Region where we experience not only the commonness of all life but the interdependence of all forms of it. We mix with the life forms as they flow, and we gain our understanding in part from personal experience. Our communities are now becoming wider, and we are more likely to live with members of our larger soul family than only those with whom we shared earthly experiences. The capacity to know ourselves as one with all living things arises from this Second Region.

It should be borne in mind that as we move from region to region we do not go anywhere in a time and space sense of the words. All of life interpenetrates, as all realms do. Our movement takes place in consciousness rather than in a time and space perspective. We have noted that as we grow in awareness we embody more and more of a single region and eventually all of the region. This does not crowd out anyone or anything else and ultimately all of creation occupies the same space but not the same consciousness of proximity. If this is difficult to understand let us look at two individuals in the same automobile. One is driving and the other is not. The longer one drives the car, the more opportunity one has to use all of one's driving skills, the more familiar one becomes with how the automobile reacts to one's skills, the more intimate a part of the machine one will feel. Likewise, the longer one remains a passenger in the automobile, the more comfortable one gets, the more one enjoys the experience, the more a part of the purpose of the auto one feels he or she has become. Further, each occupant is approximately in the same area but because of the focus each views differently all that is within and all that each passes through. By virtue of each's individual focus each rider of the automobile can be said to occupy the same point but differ in proximity to the reality of the journey. In reality our awareness can occupy the same time and space as some one else but each individual awareness would exist in its unfettered purity.

As we enter the Third Region we experience the archetypes who are transforming mental substance into soul qualities as used in the earth. Passions, instincts, desires, wishes, sensations, and feelings within the incarnate soul all arise in the Third Region of the Spirit Land. These soul qualities not only arise from this region but their expression in the earth can be seen here in their true essence. One may be startled by light storms here which give off discordant sounds and disrupt the harmony of the archetype's creation. This is the counterpart of sorrow, vengeance, and jealousy, when soul qualities are lifted up in these expressions to the Third Region.

Here in the Third Region we learn how to use the pulls

on our souls. We learn to direct our instincts and desires of every kind in a totally unselfish manner. Those who have used their aspirations as benefactors in the earth have drawn this knowledge from the Third Region of the Spirit Land. Ultimately anything of a selfish nature will be lost in the Third Region, transformed by the archetypes and sent into the earth to be used for good.

When we leave the Third Region and have rid ourselves of our last traces of any self-centeredness, we are now prepared for what Steiner described as the Fourth Region of the Spirit Land. Here we no longer participate directly in the affairs of materiality but in the care and maintenance of the archetypes in other realms. At the same time spirit from higher realms is drawn into the Fourth Region and transformed into usable substance for archetypes to work on in other lower regions. In the transformed spirit sent from the Fourth Region the very creative forces of the archetypes may be found, and even within those forces exists the pattern for creativity.

In the material world each creation is imbued with the pattern for its perfect manifestation. The pattern may be found as a fiber in the life which emanates from higher realms. It is not fed once into each living thing or even renewed periodically. As spirit, life is permanently flowing new into all living things; so too is the pattern for its perfect manifestation. As creatures in the earth we draw upon this spirit and use it to meet the daily challenges of material manifestation, as well as to build creatively in the many realms intimately connected with materiality. It must be borne in mind here that the earth is not an inferior realm. It is in fact where all realms representatively come together. There is nothing in any of the realms we experience that cannot be compared to its representation in materiality, and that includes life in the Fourth Region of the Spirit Land and beyond.

Here in the Fourth Region we find an opportunity, previously unequaled, to selflessly devote our lives to the care and maintenance of all living things that do not owe their existence to us. Those gifts for genius in arts, science, and government are drawn from the Fourth Region; one who manifests any of these talents well in the earth has previously worked in this region. If we did not pass through the Fourth Region between incarnations, we would have no interest in things common to all of humanity.

The Fifth Region of the Spirit Land is bound up mostly in intentions and purposes. Having discarded all earthly imperfections, we exercise judgment differently than we formerly had imagined possible. Now we truly fill the spirit region with our lives, loves, and hopes. In the Fifth Region prophecy is an integral, inseparable part of life; we are free to view as many of our future incarnations as we wish. If one does not experience this region between material incarnations, the person will be found to be lacking direction in the next earth life.

The Sixth and Seventh Regions of the Spirit Land are also intimately involved in creation by drawing spirit from higher realms, transforming it to be used by the archetypes for an infinite variety of manifestations in lower realms. In the Seventh Region of the Spirit Land we reach the very center of the three realities of Spirit Land, Soul Land, and Materiality. Here we live in the presence of the seeds of life which Steiner and Swedenborg called life kernels. We now recognize ourselves as our own life kernel. From the Seventh Region we have a complete view of life unfolding in each successive realm; the Spirit Land, Soul Land, and Materiality.

When in the earth, we live simultaneously in all regions of the Soul and Spirit Lands. We are not aware of our presence in other realms at the same time as we are embodied in the earth, but our lack of cognizance does not in any way inhibit our multipresence. It is from the earth that our desires, our ambitions, and what we do about them sends waves of life resonating through all regions of the Soul and Spirit Lands. As there is no time and space outside of the material universe, we have ample opportunity to experience these waves of our own soulness when we arrive in the regions where they are manifest. From the Soul and Spirit Regions we draw life as well as send it; here we experience ourselves as well as all of life.

We cannot conclude this section on realms, regions, and planes without another very brief reference to the angelic kingdom. Order is kept in all of these regions by the angelic kingdom whose countless ones we have here referred to as ministers of mercy or as ministers of grace. Angels are divided by function and there are innumerable varieties of angels. Likewise there are angels of infinite power and those of lesser power. They not only hold all realms together, their collective consciousness is essentially what each dimension is made of. We will not discuss angels or archangels any further here. Rather, a study of these sentient members of the highest order of life is best left for an entire work. It is, however, important to understand their connection with the realms we have been discussing, so the brief mention here is essential.

Chapter 4

COMPLETION

RETURN

Since taking leave of the earth plane, we have been traveling throughout many realms of reality. In each dimension we experienced that which was helpful, in some we reviewed and evaluated our experiences, but in all we were resuscitated. The realms in which we made our temporary homes and the order in which we experienced them were exactly what we needed to complete our earthly experience, to be refreshed, renewed, and prepared for our next material adventure. Each of the realms we visited were focal points from which certain basic qualities of our being emanate. We not only worked in these unique surroundings, but we mixed with the essence of each quality of which each realm was comprised. These qualities are not external things to which we responded, but they are what we are.

Our journey thus far was not meant to promote an attachment to the wonder or splendor of any particular dimension of reality. All that has been given was for the better understanding of who we really are. We are the sum total of all of our experiences from the very foundations of our beginning up until this moment. Each experience is but another thread woven into that fabric of

which we are composed. No realm is any more important than another, nor is our habitation or incarnation
into any realm more important than any other. Our experiences in reality are continuous and although certain
happenings may seem more momentous than others, it
is the accumulation of what we do with creation which
is our quest. For it is only in that accumulation of experiencing the various expressions of our God that we truly
fulfill our destiny. It is important to note that we carry all
of our experiences into each dimension because we are
the focal point of their accumulation. Further, although
each dimension operates under different sets of basic
laws, they are but variations of laws we already know.
There is one Creator, one set of principles of life we call
laws, and one direction in which to grow. The infinite variety in creation is largely due to the limitless ways in
which the same things may be manifest. If we would just
watch the patterns of what we know unfold before us,
we would see ever so clearly the most important aspects
of what seems both behind and ahead of us. Now with
what we have in hand let us turn our attention toward
our inevitable return to materiality.

Those who feel their material experiences were cut
short before fulfillment will naturally return before those
who were satisfied that they accomplished approximately what they had incarnated into materiality to
achieve. Many who died young, who died unexpectedly,
who believe they did not have an ample opportunity to
experience their life in the earth will, for better or worse,
travel a more abbreviated route through reality before
their return. This limited renewal may have an indelible
influence on their next material incarnation, leaving
them insufficiently armed for what they are about to encounter. Also such a short recovery from their last earthly
life and an eagerness for a quick return often limits one's
choices, and this may result in a regrettable error. We

must not overlook the fact that one who died younger often does not need the review and renewal to the same extent as one who may have lived in the earth many years longer. Both Cayce and Steiner agree that insufficient preparation for return to an earthly incarnation is far more common with those who died before they expected they would than with those who lived long lives in the earth.

As we discussed, there is a certain order in which we move through realms and that order is dictated by sympathetic resonance as well as proximity. Sympathetic resonance is the overriding factor in our journey through reality, and proximity is the shading influence. The timing for our return is first and foremost a personal choice, while the influence which makes this a longer or shorter, a more difficult or easier journey is proximity. All throughout our spiritual journey between earthly incarnations we live and grow in communities with those we consider to be our soul family, with whom we have shared experiences. There is no level of reality where we do not have members of this soul family of ours, and we commune with them wherever in creation we go. We even plan together for our next incarnation and this of course greatly influences our return. We do not plan our return with certain members of our soul family simply because we like them or they like us. Such plans are conceived because of karmic considerations and because such a relationship is vital to what we hope will be accomplished in our next earthly life.

One does not sit down at a certain point in creation, take a view of what is in the earth, assisted or otherwise, weigh the options, and make an instant decision regarding their next incarnation. We do not make informed decisions in the earth that way nor do we do so outside of the earth. We take into consideration relationships with those who have preceded us into materiality as well as those who will follow. It would be foolish to think that decisions of such magnitude for each of us would be so poorly planned. Such a choice is made little by little as one grows in reality, and the final step is a small one indeed. Gradual planning to be part of a family unit, a community, and a nation takes place over what we would conceive of as time from an earthly perspective. The Edgar Cayce discourses make a very strong case, insisting that we choose our families, our parents, and even make agreements, where possible, to choose our spouses and children. This is not to infer that changes in plans will not occur, but we should be aware of the vast amount of planning that is done before our earthly incarnation.

When we are making most of our plans and agreements for our next incarnation, we do not have physical details before us. Instead we have before us relationships to others, to situations, and to those forces which have prepared us.

In our decision-making process about our next material incarnation we deal largely with two factors. First we work with motivation, then with potential, and all the rest is the great adventure we call life. Let us not think that we incarnate for the adventure alone. For life and its living can be just as exciting for all who incarnate whatever their goals may be. For life to be truly constructive we must deal with the motivation and potentials which are best for us at the time; thus we not only experience the adventure our God has prepared for us, but we do so for our greatest good. As we move through the realms around the earth, motivation is laid bare before us. Soon it is the most obvious condition and the framer of all experience. We learn to identify motivation very easily and accept it as the creative essence of the soul. Respect for this primal motivational cause becomes inescapable early on in our journey between earth lives,

and we learn that motivation is the first condition in reality. In the realm ruled by cause and effect, motivation
is the fulcrum through whose action all things come into
being.

Potential is that inevitable unfolding of reality, once
motivation is acted upon. Where there is no time or
space, potential in all of its glory is the ever present now.
In those higher realms to which we resonate, potential
becomes so much a part of our experience that we do
not separate it from motivation. Instead, potential and
motivation become as opposite poles of the same reality. If we would have a more accurate understanding of
potential, we must understand that it is multifaceted.
For example, if we were to help someone overcome a
condition, we must consider how it would affect that
person, how it may change the lives around the individual, and how ultimately it would affect all of reality.
This compound view of a single act is what the Jewish
mystics call branches, and potential most certainly
branches out in all directions. So astute do we become
in understanding potential outside of materiality that
ultimately we view not only the branches as they reach
out in one dimension but their expression in multiple
dimensions at the same time. Now we have a more accurate understanding of the all-encompassing reality of
potential.

Motivation may naturally change once we are deeply
involved in materiality, and potential will of necessity
likewise change. This is part of what makes life such an
exciting adventure, and why shouldn't it be? In those
realms to which we took flight following our earthly incarnation we reviewed our activities and measured them
against the potential for which we incarnated. The results, whether we received them positively or negatively,
were etched in our memories. The memories we have in
regard to our successes or failures, in having achieved

the potential in our last earthly incarnation, guide us in making those numerous and gradual decisions regarding our next incarnation. As we move through realms in community with our soul family, we make certain decisions based on a clearer knowledge of motivation, potential, and the karma that will help us bridge the two. For it is in karma, a limited form of grace, that we find that strength necessary to successfully carry the weight of material experience as it bears down upon us day by day.

There is no productive relationship where all parties cannot gain equally. Some relationships though are more opportune at certain times than others. The ability to deal constructively with any one person or any group depends largely on preparation, and we are not prepared to meet every thing at once. Likewise, certain conditions have more constructive potential for us than others, also because of preparation. Further, certain time periods are far more beneficial for our earthly incarnation than others, because of the material realm's proximity to those dimensions from which we have drawn the strengths we need the most.

So here we have it; we made plans bit by bit as we traveled through reality, regarding our next material incarnation, and we were drawn to the proper timing just as we were drawn by correspondence to the realms to which we resonate. When the proximity is correct, when conditions are best, we then make a final decision and in so doing we gain immeasurably. Half the gain in life is "showing up"; consequently, according to Edgar Cayce, half the gain in an earthly incarnation is in deciding to do it. Throughout the whole of the experience the angels of grace are there to give us all that we have need of at any time. They are likewise ever present to help us in our decisions regarding our next material incarnation.

There are those of us who have so squandered our

opportunities that we do not have the fullness of freedom as do others. In such situations our route through spiritual realms is not full enough to enjoy the lessons which would be learned by a slower, more wholesome period of recovery. As a result, some of us cannot clearly see motivation and potential while others of us may not even care. There are those of the angelic ministry who guide such myopic souls toward their next incarnation, but it is ever the decision of the individual to incarnate or not.

Now let us look at the obvious question of what would happen if one of these myopic souls refused to reincarnate into the earth plane when it was necessary. What would happen if a soul simply said no, I will not go. Understanding the nature of free will, we must accept that no one is forced to incarnate against his or her choice. All will be assisted to reconsider; they will be taken to realms and be revitalized in every way appropriate for their awakening. There is no earthly time frame in which such assistance can take place; it could be one year, one thousand years, or tens of thousands of years. If when all that can be done is done and the tormented soul simply refuses to go on, that soul is then mercifully absorbed into the whole. Once absorbed, the soul's individuality is eternally lost, the soul no longer exists as a life force with a destiny of its own, and this is the "banishment" referred to in Judeo-Christian texts. This is also touched upon in the Cayce discourses when he said that "the *individuality* of the soul that separates itself is lost." (826-8)

We have now the decision to reincarnate; the soul begins to move through reality. The focus becomes narrower and narrower as the movement continues. As we move closer to materiality we see the potentials better and how close they are in keeping with what we expected when we started to make the many decisions necessary regarding this incarnation. At first we see activities elevated spiritually and work with this. But the closer we move to the primal causes in the earth, the more detail and color are filled in for us. We now begin to view conditions in a more material perspective and evaluate some differently. When we first began our return, we may have experienced conditions in the earth in terms of celestial harmonies, then as we moved closer we observed the same experiences in heavenly colors, then in emotions, and finally in viewing the very activities themselves.

It should be said that this viewing of material activities is not something easy, although it is common. There are those angels and their helpers who have given their whole being to communication, and they lend themselves as a bridge so that incarnating souls may see in the minutest detail the activities into which they have chosen to incarnate. Such an observation could last several years, but it is more likely to last less than one full year. In this condition the incarnating soul can influence activity, as do angels, by force of the impressions they may make on the emotions of those already incarnate. Those who are not yet incarnate cannot influence the unfolding of events in the earth by cause and effect. We often think that incarnating souls hover around us, influencing all sorts of things, that they are aware of everything and can cause changes more easily than we can. In fact the incarnating soul can change nothing except to influence those in the earth to make changes; there is little in the earth of interest to the incarnating soul that does not involve its individual path at that time.

When the time is right and conditions are proper, the leap will be made from what we consider the spiritual to the material. Let us think of how such a leap would take place. A musician playing a beautiful piece of music is fully aware of being a trained musical artist. Such persons have mastered certain proficiency in playing music on their instrument, and they are likewise aware of the techniques available to them. They have first chosen to be a musician, and by many subsequent decisions have chosen their preferred instrument, the type of music they favor, the style in which they like to perform, and literally dozens of equally important factors. As musicians play, they become more and more focused on the harmonies, the melody, and the rhythm. Soon they are so focused that they are indeed the music, and it resonates through every part of their consciousness. Incarnating souls parallel this focus and literally become part of the material realm as it resonates through them; like a musician, they lose sight of all that led up to this magnificent symphony. Correspondence, karma, and choice now propel an incarnating soul from one realm into the other. Our consciousness will be absorbed with materiality, and we will thus be tied to the earth plane. The concert hall has been rented, the orchestra assembled on stage, the conductor takes his or her place in full view of the musicians, the soloist walks out to center stage, and we are ready to begin again.

EPILOGUE

In the preface to this work it was our stated purpose to awaken in our readers a sense of their own immortality, through a better understanding of the continuity of life in all realms—particularly the connectedness of life in the material to life in the spiritual. More poetically stated, our purpose was to awaken in each the realization of the oneness of life and death. Consequently, knowledge without use is more of a detriment than it is a help. In psychic discourse 5753-2, trying to impress those present with the urgent need to apply knowledge, the entranced Cayce stated, "Do not gain knowledge only to thine undoing. Remember Adam." In the same discourse Cayce cautioned those who would give information without thinking of its application, when he said, "Do not attempt to force, impel or to even try to impress thy knowledge upon another. Remember what the serpent did to Eve." We hope that, as was our purpose, we have awakened a sense of immortality in the reader. Consequently, we are compelled to start readers down the path where they may apply in their daily life whatever has been awakened.

In the introduction we referred to the shadows that

obscure true reality. If we are willing to see in the light of where we are, we will indeed know what lies in the shadows beyond our vision. We need only two qualities to succeed: one is honest inquiry and the other is a willingness to act on what we find.

How then are we to relate what we see to what is beyond the light of where we are? Once we do finally recognize what lies in the reality beyond, how are we to apply it in our current circumstances? The answer to both questions is correspondence. Correspondence goes far beyond emblems or symbols. Correspondence is the inclusive relationship of all subsequent manifestations of the same thing. For the sake of clarity let us expand on our definition of correspondence. A single product of primal creation is manifest in all subsequent, less primal realms. So inseparable are these varied manifestations that to affect one is to affect them all. Correspondence does not deal with reflections; it deals with original creation, manifest in appropriate form, throughout every level of reality.

We would like to set out here a methodology for understanding and using correspondence. It is not our purpose to compile a massive catalog of what corresponds to what. Although it is natural for us, as seekers, to prefer such a directory, with such a list we will ultimately gain little ability to search for ourselves. Without a personal, meaningful search we will inhibit our understanding as well as our success in applying what we find. An honest, organized effort at working with correspondence will yield an understanding of our own omnipresence, our connectedness with all life everywhere. With such an understanding we may begin to discover the oneness of life and death.

Why should an all-loving God consign us to a seemingly mediocre realm such as materiality, when we could be assisting the unfolding of creation? Why do we choose to return to such a narrow existence over and over again, after resonating to the Music of the Spheres? Because the laws of cause and effect are fundamental in the material dimension, we can cause things to happen and subsequently we can experience the result. "In the beginning the Lord created the Heavens and the earth," He gave them their marching orders, and by virtue of His presence in all things He experiences the results. By correspondence we reach across multiple realms, and we cause change throughout creation from this narrow consciousness we occupy in materiality. It is from our lives in the earth that we build our place in other realms; cause and effect are our bricks and correspondence is our mortar. It is worth repeating that the countless levels of reality have the same essential cause. Thus, life manifest in each dimension reflects a more primal creation which preexisted it in yet higher realms. Not only are higher realms reflected in the earth but they do so in their entirety. They do so by correspondence. This synthesis is unique in its scope.

Let us take a brief look at the law of cause and effect as it reaches across time. As life from higher realms is expressed in material dimensions, we act upon it. Emanuel Swedenborg noted that by our activity we transform material life; we inevitably transform that which exists in spirit into that to which it corresponds. The transformation which takes place in spirit is subsequently expressed in materiality by means of correspondence, as we experience our own creation. Correspondence is really a simple concept that offers a good explanation of how creativity travels in all directions across the face of reality.

Each realm has a higher and lower dimension. Emanuel Swedenborg refers to the higher as the internal and the lower dimension as the external. The internal corresponds to the will, which is creative, and the external corresponds to the mind, which is formed by the will. As was emphasized in previous chapters, the will precedes the mind, which essentially is the byproduct, the result of the will's activity upon spirit. A good example is Swedenborg's statement that fire corresponds to love while light corresponds to truth. Love burns clean, it warms creation, it is the essence of all manifest life. Taking the Cayce, Steiner, and Swedenborg philosophies one step further, love properly applied, in accord with the pattern imprinted within it, is truth. The meaning here should not be missed, so it bears restating. Love is the fundamental essence of all that has been created, and truth is the lawful expression of the essence. Thus, whether we see it or not, the lawful application of love will light the way for us all. Swedenborg saw that love and truth are bound together as are fire and light by the angels of God, who travel between these two realities, holding them in place. This is not only holding together the two poles such as love and truth as well as fire and light but their connection with corresponding form as well.

The literary style of the Old Testament is that of correspondence. To understand the unique mode of expression employed in the Old Testament, the student will find that both the written and oral laws of those who originally authored these books excluded abstract form. Instead, the universal was explained by that in materiality to which it corresponded. Through the common everyday use of our language, one can easily miss the spiritual correspondence in the ancient Hebraic writings because those texts abound with dated idiomatic expressions. Nonetheless, if we wish to understand the Old Testament on a level other than historical, we must read it through the lens of correspondence. When we go beyond mere symbolism, we will then begin to see universal truth expressed as elevated material concepts. To understand the Old Testament books of the Bible is to understand correspondence and vice versa.

Nowhere can the seeker find more graphic illustrations of correspondence than in the works of Emanuel Swedenborg. His *Heaven and Its Wonders and Hell from Things Heard and Seen* is a veritable blueprint for correspondence. He observed that spirituality and materiality are conjoined by the soul of humanity. Everywhere we look in the earth we see correspondence as material things are joined to spiritual things through each of us. Let us be very clear here how we, our souls, are the conjunction between matter and spirit, as we take a closer look at our physical bodies which are manifestations of our souls.

The Edgar Cayce psychic discourses noted that all of creation is reflected in our material universe and that the entire universe is expressed in our physical bodies. If we follow this line of thought, we may conclude that all creation can be found in our physical bodies. Correspondence explains the relationship we have to higher creation and its presence within us in physical form.

Swedenborg noted that love, intelligence, and joy correspond to our head. Love is the primal essence from which all things come and this naturally corresponds to our crown. We may not think lovingly or even of love, but the fact that we think at all is a manifestation of love. Intelligence is an ordered and confined form of consciousness expressed in three-dimensional reality, while joy is more a spiritual manifestation of love. All that we do must express love both joyfully and reasonably. If we do not integrate these aspects of our own crown, we distort life by an overbalance of one at the expense of the other. Further, chaos and confusion, on both a spiritual and material basis, are the likely result in the absence of joy and reason.

Faith and charity correspond to the breast; they are the heart and lungs of the soul. Faith pulsates throughout our being so that the love it propels may resuscitate every part of our being. Charity is like the breath of the body, in that it supplies the fuel necessary to energize the cells of our being. One cannot have charity if they do not possess faith, and in the absence of both, the breath of life in an individual is impeded physically, mentally, and spiritually.

Devotion to others as in marriage is a basis upon which we rest. Further, union connects foundations to our highest motivations. We do not use the term rest as idleness, but to explain that our highest motivations find their seat in union. Taking this all into account one can see why devotion to others corresponds to the loin of the individual. Love, joy, reason, faith, and charity must find their seat in devotion to others. This will result in a free flow of life in our spiritual body, our mental body, and our physical body.

The natural underside of love is truth, thus truth corresponds to the feet. In properly applying those attributes outlined here, the natural result is truth. It is in such an application of love that we find our most solid foundation. The firmness of our foundation is directly proportionate with how well we have applied what we know.

We see by illustration how we can act on material relationships and change their corresponding spiritual manifestations. Let us now look at a simple case of correspondence and how we can bring things of spiritual import into materiality, act upon them, and change them. A musical instrument is designed through form and used to play music; when done properly, it brings a high form of universal harmony into materiality. What we hear with our ears is actually conjoined to the Music of the Spheres or harmony of creation. The musician is the means of conjunction. When the musician lends an individual style to what is being played, the harmony is added both in- and outside of materiality. Consequently, the individual musical expression is now a permanent part of the resonance. The fact that the physical music ceases when the musician stops playing does not mean that the universal harmony, which has been added to, will ever stop.

We must consider several things when viewing the correspondence to what we encounter in our first estate after death. Because we are acting upon the earthly correspondence, we are naturally drawn to those environs after death where we invested so much of our attention in material life. It is much like playing all of the positions on a baseball team. We throw the ball, race to the batter's box, pick up the bat, and hit the ball. We run to the outfield, we catch the ball, and we are out. Before incarnating we are throwing the ball or setting in motion those opportunities upon which we will act in the earth. Following our birth in materiality we hit the ball or act upon those opportunities we previously set in motion. After death we go to where the ball will land and we catch it as the natural result of where our earthly activities must be met. All along we are dealing with continuous events in a string of connected, corresponding activities.

Once again, it is not our intent to build a list of correspondence. It is, however, our purpose to encourage the reader to reason correspondence. The reasoning process is in and of itself a spiritual activity. Thus it will awaken far more essential understanding than any list of what corresponds to what. Only through such a process can inquirers purposefully reach out across reality and more fully understand, by their own experiences, their oneness with all creation.

Bibliography

Association for Research and Enlightenment, Inc. Edgar Cayce Library Series. (Vol. 1), *Life and Death,* 1973. (2) *Meditation, Part I,* 1974. (3), *Meditation, Part II,* 1975. (4), *Dreams and Dreaming, Part I,* 1976. (5), *Dreams and Dreaming, Part II,* 1976. (6), *Early Christian Epic,* 1976. (7), *The Study Group Readings,* 1977. (8), *Psychic Development,* 1978. (9), *Psychic Awareness,* 1979. (10), *Jesus the Pattern,* 1980. (11), *Christ Consciousness,* 1980. (12), *Daily Living,* 1981. (13), *Attitudes and Emotions, Part I,* 1981. (14), *Attitudes and Emotions, Part II,* 1982. (15), *Attitudes and Emotions, Part III,* 1982. (16), *Expanded Search for God, Part I,* 1983. (17), *Expanded Search for God, Part II,* 1983. (18), *Astrology, Part I,* 1985. (19), *Astrology, Part II,* 1985. (20), *Mind,* 1986. (21), *Soul Development,* 1986. (22), *Atlantis,* 1987. (23), Egypt, *Part I,* 1989. (24), Egypt, *Part II,* 1989. Virginia Beach, Va.; A.R.E. Press.

Association for Research and Enlightenment, Inc. *The Edgar Cayce Readings.* Edgar Cayce Foundation, Virginia Beach, Va., 1973.

Bro, Harmon Hartzell. *Dreams in the Life of Prayer.* Harper and Row, New York, N.Y., 1970.

Bro, Harmon Hartzell. *Edgar Cayce on Religion and Psychic Experience.* Paperback Library, New York, N.Y., 1970.

Bro, Harmon Hartzell. *Seer Out of Season, A: The Life of Edgar Cayce.* New American Library, New York, N.Y., 1989.

Buber, Martin. *I and Thou.* Charles Scribner's Sons, New York, N.Y., 1970.

Carey, Ken. *Starseed, the Third Millennium.* Harper Collins, New York, N.Y., 1987.

Drummond, Richard H. *A Life of Jesus the Christ.* Harper and Row, New York, N.Y., 1989.

Ford, Arthur, and Bro, Margueritte Harmon. *Nothing So Strange.* Harper and Row, New York, N.Y., 1958.

Greaves, Helen. *Testimony of Light*. Neville Spearman Publishers, The C.W. Daniel Company, Ltd., Essex, England, 1969.

Hudson, Thomson Jay. *The Law of Psychic Phenomena*. Hudson-Cohan Publishing Co., Salinas, Cal., 1977.

James, William. *The Varieties of Religious Experience*. The Modern Library, New York, N.Y., 1936.

Kübler-Ross, Elisabeth. *Death, the Final Stage of Growth*. Prentice Hall, Engelwood Cliffs, N.J., 1975.

Kübler-Ross, Elisabeth. *On Death and Dying*. Macmillan Publishing Company, New York, N.Y., 1969.

Macmillan, Dorothy. *To Hear the Angels Sing*. Mornington Press, Issaquah, Wash., 1988.

McArthur, Bruce. *Universal Laws: An A.R.E. Tape Seminar*. Association for Research and Enlightenment, Inc., Virginia Beach, Va., 1980.

Montgomery, Ruth. *Here and Hereafter*. Fawcet Publications, Inc., Greenwich, Conn., 1968.

Moody, Raymond A., Jr. *Life After Life*. Bantam Books, New York, N.Y., 1975.

Nolan, Albert. *Jesus Before Christianity*. Orbis Books, Maryknoll, N.Y., 1976.

Ouspensky, P.D. *Tertium Organum*. Vantage Books, New York, N.Y., 1920.

Puryear, Meredith Ann. *Healing Through Meditation and Prayer*. A.R.E. Press, Virginia Beach, Va., 1978.

Reed, Henry. *Awakening Your Psychic Powers*. Harper and Row, San Francisco, Cal., 1988.

Ritchie, George G., Jr. *My Life After Dying*. Hampton Roads Publishing Co., Virginia Beach, Va., 1991.

Sanderfur, Glenn. *Lives of the Master: The Rest of the Jesus Story*. A.R.E. Press, Virginia Beach, Va., 1988.

Scholem, Gershom. *Kabbalah*. The New American Library, New York, N.Y., 1974.

Sechrist, Elsie. *Dreams—Your Magic Mirror.* Cowles Education Corporation, New York, N.Y., 1968.

Steiner, Rudolf. *Life Between Death and Rebirth.* Anthroposophic Press, Hudson, N.Y., 1968.

Steiner, Rudolf. *Theosophy.* Anthroposophic Press, Hudson, N.Y., 1971.

Steinsaltz, Adin. *The Strife of the Spirit.* Jason Aronson, Inc., Northpage, N.Y., 1988.

Steinsaltz, Adin. *The Thirteen Petalled Rose.* Basic Books, Inc., New York, N.Y., 1980.

Swedenborg, Emanuel. *Angelic Wisdom Concerning Divine Love.* Swedenborg Foundation, London, England, 1964.

Swedenborg, Emanuel. *Heaven and Its Wonders and Hell from Things Heard and Seen.* Swedenborg Foundation, London, England, 1964.

Taylor, Ruth Mattson. *Witness from Beyond.* Forward Books, White Plains, N.Y., 1975.

The Holy Bible. King James Version. Thomas Nelson, Inc., New York, N.Y., 1972.

World Book Encyclopedia. World Books, Inc., Chicago Ill. 1982.

You Can Receive Books Like This One and Much, Much More

You can begin to receive books in the *A.R.E. Membership Series* and many more benefits by joining the non-profit Association for Research and Enlightenment, Inc., as a Sponsoring or Life member.

The A.R.E. has a worldwide membership that receives a wide variety of study aids, all aimed at assisting individuals in their spiritual, mental, and physical growth.

Every member of A.R.E. receives a copy of *Venture Inward*, the organization's bimonthly magazine; a periodic in-depth journal, *The New Millennium;* opportunity to borrow, through the mail, from a collection of more than 500 files on medical and metaphysical subjects; access to one of the world's most complete libraries on metaphysical and spiritual subjects; and opportunities to participate in conferences, international tours, a retreat-camp for children and adults, and numerous nationwide volunteer activities.

In addition to the foregoing benefits, Sponsoring and Life members also receive as gifts three books each year in the *A.R.E. Membership Series.*

If you are interested in finding out more about membership in A.R.E. and the many benefits that can assist you on your path to fulfillment, you can easily contact the Membership Department by writing Membership, A.R.E., P.O. Box 595, Virginia Beach, VA 23451-0595 or by calling **1-800-333-4499** or faxing **1-757-422-6921**.

**Explore our electronic visitor's center on the Internet:
http://www.are-cayce.com**